Praise for *The Most Powerful Saints in Exorcisms*

"Charles D. Fraune and Patrick O'Hearn have done an excellent job covering the subject of saints and exorcisms. As an exorcist, I have witnessed, again and again, the importance and power of the saints in exorcisms. It's no wonder that the Litany of the Saints is one of the very first and essential parts of the Rite of Exorcism. This is a book every exorcist should read, but it's also a book for all to come to realize the importance of the Communion of Saints in our lives. A day should not pass without our invoking and thanking this great choir of saints and their powerful labors on our behalf. We pray that one day we will join their august company."

—**Msgr. Stephen J. Rossetti**, Author, *My Confrontation with Hell* and *Diary of an American Exorcist*; President, St. Michael Center for Spiritual Renewal

"This book will prove to be a valuable resource in the world of exorcism. God does not want anyone to suffer alone, and the saints are valuable allies in combating Satan and the other fallen angels. The halos the saints wear are reflections of the glory of God, and that is a light that will cause demons to flee. We need to rely on their intercession."

—**Fr. Vincent Lampert**, Former exorcist, Archdiocese of Indianapolis

"Demons in exorcisms call saints 'assassins.' *The Most Powerful Saints in Exorcisms* is not your typical exorcism book. While it includes extraordinary stories that will capture your attention, its deeper aim is to reveal the saints as fierce warriors in the battle for souls. After reading this book, you will never think of our blessed saints the same way again. You'll see these holy men and women as Heaven's special forces—active, present, and powerful. May you read this book and come to rely more on the great cloud of witnesses to help you as you walk the narrow way to your place in Heaven."

—**Dan Burke**, Author, *The Devil in the Castle*

"This book is timely, relevant, and edifying. As a member of an exorcist's team who, for the past eighteen years, has assisted in countless exorcisms, I attest to the reality and beauty of the contents of this book. Having worked with most of the exorcists represented here, I am grateful for their shared insights. Readers will discover faith-affirming truths about the power of the saints, who actively labor as God's ambassadors to defeat demons and to defend God's children. I highly recommend this book, especially for Catholic families."

—**Kathleen Beckman**, Speaker and
Author, *A Family Guide to Spiritual Warfare*

The Most Powerful
Saints in Exorcisms

Also by Patrick O'Hearn
from Sophia Institute Press

Our Lady of Sorrows
Nursery of Heaven (co-author)
The Truth about Hell (co-author)
Sacred Heart of Jesus

THE MOST *POWERFUL* SAINTS IN EXORCISMS

What Exorcists Want You to Know

CHARLES D. FRAUNE *and*
PATRICK O'HEARN

SOPHIA INSTITUTE PRESS
Manchester, New Hampshire

*A saint keeps watch over his country and
obtains its salvation. His prayers and virtues
are more powerful than all the armies in the world.*

—St. Peter Julian Eymard

Contents

Appendices

Acknowledgments

We would like to thank our spouses for their unfailing support, and our children for allowing us to sacrifice time with them to write this book.

We would like to thank our parents for their faithful witness.

We would like to thank all of the exorcists who allowed us to interview them or share the fruits of their labors. Thank you for leading us into battle and tirelessly handing on the Sacred Traditions of our Catholic Faith.

We would like to thank Sophia Institute Press, especially President Charlie McKinney, managing editor Anna Maria Dube, editorial assistant Caleb Selecter, marketing manager Molly Rublee, associate director of publicity Sarah Lemieux, publicity coordinator Sammy Hughes, and our editor, Laura Bement, for publishing this important work.

Finally and most importantly, we give thanks to God, Our Lady, the saints, and the holy angels for inspiring this work.

We pray that *The Most Powerful Saints in Exorcisms* increases your love for God and His saints.

About the Exorcists

This book features teachings and statements from the following exorcists (listed alphabetically):

- † **Servant of God Fr. Candido Amantini, C.P.,** was a Passionist priest and Rome's exorcist for thirty-six years. He was the spiritual mentor to Fr. Gabriele Amorth. He died in 1992.
- † **Fr. Gabriele Amorth** was a renowned Italian exorcist and the founder of the International Association of Exorcists. He is the author of numerous books. He died in 2016.
- † **Fr. Francesco Bamonte** is an Italian priest, exorcist, and author. He is a member of the Servants of the Immaculate Heart of Mary. He is the president of the International Association of Exorcists (IAE), an organization that supports priests involved in exorcism and related spiritual ministries.
- † **Fr. Vincent Lampert** is the former exorcist for the Archdiocese of Indianapolis, Indiana, and an author.
- † **Fr. Chad Ripperger** is an exorcist for the Archdiocese of Denver, Colorado, and the founder of the Doloran

Fathers. His apostolate also includes the organization Sensus Traditionis, which hosts many of his conferences and books.

† **Msgr. Stephen J. Rossetti** is the senior exorcist for the Archdiocese of Washington, the founder of the St. Michael Center for Spiritual Renewal, and an author.

† **Fr. John Szada** is an exorcist for the Diocese of Harrisburg, Pennsylvania.

We also consulted with several exorcists who chose to remain anonymous. They will be referenced by the following pseudonyms:

† **Fr. Alphonsus** is a diocesan exorcist.

† **Fr. Athanasius** is a diocesan exorcist.

† **Fr. Benedict** is an exorcist in a religious community.

† **Fr. Pius** is an exorcist in a religious community.

† **Fr. Timothy** is a diocesan exorcist.

Finally, we also worked with **Adam Blai**, layman, peritus of religious demonology and exorcism for the Diocese of Pittsburgh, Pennsylvania, and notable author and speaker on the deliverance ministry.

Introduction

On a typical Wednesday morning in St. Peter's Square, an extraordinary event took place—one that went largely unnoticed by the world yet one that revealed the power of God working through His saints. Fr. Gabriele Amorth, one of the most recognized exorcists to ever live, often called Rome's Exorcist or the Pope's Exorcist, took a possessed girl named Sabrina to a papal audience. The girl needed to be held down by ten people. St. John Paul II, the pope at the time, immediately noticed Sabrina and asked his secretary to bring her to him so he could help her out of sight of the rest of the people. " 'No, no, leave me alone. Leave me alone!' she shouts. The pope exorcises her on the spot. He blesses her several times and then lets her be,"[1] recounts Fr. Amorth. While Sabrina would be liberated a few years later, Fr. Amorth believed that "the exorcism performed by Wojtyla left its mark on her."[2]

---

[1] Quoted in Domenico Agasso, *Fr. Gabriele Amorth: Rome's Exorcist*, trans. Bret Thoman, OFS (Gastonia, NC: Tan Books, 2023), 173.

[2] Quoted in Agasso, *Fr. Gabriele Amorth*, 174.

St. Peter Julian Eymard reminds us that the saints' "prayers and virtues are more powerful than all the armies in the world."[3] Saints have converted thousands of souls, including some of the Church's fiercest persecutors. They have stood unflinching, face-to-face, with some of the most evil governments and ideologies. Communism, liberalism, socialism, and numerous heresies have come and gone—yet the saints remain. The saints have left their mark on souls, and they continue, in the words of St. Thérèse of Lisieux, to "spend [their] Heaven in doing good upon earth."[4] Not even Satan and all his forces of evil have been able to stand up to the saints. Some saints have banished the devil in exorcisms, and others have offered spiritual freedom by their prayers, their blessings, and their words of encouragement.

While Satan and his minions seek to drag every soul into the fires of Hell, the saints desire to bring each one of us to the Beatific Vision. Christ alone is the One who ultimately delivers any soul from possession, yet the saints are images of Christ and continue His work until the end of the world. Therefore, just as Christ exorcised demons during His earthly ministry, so His saints cast out evil spirits in His name even to this day. Saints are so powerful in their work against the devil that St. Thomas Aquinas even posited that the saints will fill the empty seats in Heaven left by the fallen angels.[5]

---

[3] St. Peter Julian Eymard, *The Real Presence: Eucharistic Meditations* (New York: Sentinel Press, 1938), 22.

[4] St. Thérèse of Lisieux, *The Story of a Soul* (Charlotte, NC: Tan Books, 2010), 174.

[5] St. Thomas Aquinas, *Summa Theologica* I, q. 63, art. 9; in *The Summa Theologiae of St. Thomas Aquinas*, trans. Fathers of the English Dominican Province, 2nd ed. (1920); available at *New Advent* (Kevin Knight, 2017), https://www.newadvent.org/summa/.

Fr. Vincent Lampert described best what happens when a saint appears during an exorcism:

> The best analogy would be to think of a room that has bugs in it. You will walk into it and then you turn on the light. What do the bugs do? They scurry because they can't be in the light. Somebody that's been trapped in a cave for days and steps out into the light: they can't look at it, it's almost blinding. That's what, I think, the saints do when they arrive during an exorcism, during the Litany of the Saints, when they're called upon: they bring the glory of God with them and that brightness, you could say, is blinding to the demons. Then the demons want to scurry and get away like those bugs that are crawling back into the cracks and the crevices.[6]

Throughout this book, we will share the testimonies of several exorcists who tell their true stories of the most powerful saints in exorcisms, and we will explore why these saints appear during exorcisms. It is clear that God has chosen some saints to have an influential role in exorcisms, and we are able to highlight some of them here. Given the private nature of exorcism, however, we could only interview a select group of exorcists, so the stories we could hear about the saints' involvement in exorcisms were limited. We respect the need for privacy in exorcisms, yet we are sure that had we been able to speak with more exorcists, we would have learned about the involvement of even more saints. Servant of God Fr. Candido Amantini, C.P., the exorcist for the Diocese of Rome for thirty-six years

---

[6] Fr. Vincent Lampert, in discussion with Patrick O'Hearn, August 2024.

and the beloved mentor of Fr. Gabriele Amorth, conveyed the following to his protégé:

> One exorcist by naming Padre Pio can provoke a strong reaction in the possessed, while another exorcist in naming him may not have any effect whatsoever. You have to find your own way. It will be your way. Always remember St. Leopold Mandic. He lived in Padua. He heard confessions all day long. Often exorcists called on him for help. He would arrive, attend the exorcism in silence, and then would intervene at the end, saying, "Out, out. Go away." And the spellbound devil would disappear. That was his way. You, too, must find yours.[7]

As we read about the various saints and their roles in exorcisms, we must remember that the saints are given to us by God to be our most powerful friends and intercessors. Some of these saints were exorcists. Some were even possessed by demons at various times in their lives. But in the end, every saint battled Satan and was victorious with God's help. Indeed, after Jesus and Mary, the saints are the greatest enemies of Satan and his fallen angels. And so the saints continue to show up in exorcisms in a very commanding way, since, in the words of Msgr. Stephen Rossetti, "In an exorcism, we enter the supernatural realm of the angels and saints."[8] We would be wise to always seek the saints' aid so that we might keep ourselves, and all we love, fortified against Satan, and so that we might ultimately join them in Heaven, for as God promises us, "be faithful unto death, and I will give you the crown of life" (Rev. 2:10).

---

[7] Quoted in Agasso, *Fr. Gabriele Amorth*, 129.

[8] Msgr. Stephen J. Rossetti, *Diary of an American Exorcist: Demons, Possession, and the Modern-Day Battle against Ancient Evil* (Manchester, NH: Sophia Institute Press, 2021), 175.

1

The Power of the
Communion of Saints

"Let God arise, and let His enemies be scattered: and let them that hate Him flee from before His face" (Ps. 67:2, Douay-Rheims). Thus begins the Mass in honor of Sts. Marius, Martha, Audifax, and Abachum, martyrs of the third century, as well as the Mass in honor of St. Michael the Archangel, the chief of the heavenly hosts. In this introit, the opening scriptural verse and prayer for the Mass that sets the tone for the proper feast of the day, we hear of the power that flows through the intercession of the saints. This power has been made manifest in the experiences of the faithful throughout the two-thousand-year history of the Church, especially through the lives and stories of exorcists.

The great exorcist, Fr. Gabriele Amorth, said, "The saints in heaven intercede for us with great power and efficacy. We must pray to them often."[9] His recommendation speaks in unison with the mind of the Church, which stated in 1563 at the Ecumenical Council of Trent:

---

[9] Fr. Gabriele Amorth, *An Exorcist Explains the Demonic: The Antics of Satan and His Army of Fallen Angels*, trans. Charlotte J. Fasi (Manchester, NH: Sophia Institute Press, 2016), 125.

The saints who reign together with Christ offer up their prayers to God for men, [and] it is good and beneficial suppliantly to invoke them and to have recourse to their prayers, aid, (and) help for obtaining benefits from God, through His Son, Jesus Christ our Lord, who alone is our Redeemer and Savior.[10]

The saints, with us, and with the souls in Purgatory, together make up the Church in her three states: the Church Militant on earth, the Church Suffering in Purgatory, and the Church Triumphant in Heaven. These three states are in communion with each other in the Mystical Body of Christ. As a result, graces flow from one stage to the other: those in Heaven pour out the abundance of grace to us on earth through their intercession, and we offer our own spiritual goods and merits for those brethren undergoing their purification in Purgatory. Fr. Amorth said that through this communion, "an intense exchange of spiritual benefits takes place ... [and] our weakness is greatly helped by their fraternal solicitude."[11]

This recourse to the saints is present throughout the devotional life of Catholics: in the Holy Rosary, on the feasts of the saints, in the naming of our children, during novenas to the saints, in imitating the saints, in reading about the lives of the saints, and even in the Holy Sacrifice of the Mass, during which we invoke the names of specific saints and join with all of Heaven

---

[10] Council of Trent, Session 25, "On the Invocation, Veneration, and Relics of Saints, and on Sacred Images," December 3–4, 1563; in *The Council of Trent*, ed. and trans. J. Waterworth (London: Dolman, 1848); available at www.papalencyclicals.net/councils /trent.htm.

[11] Amorth, *An Exorcist Explains the Demonic*, 125.

in praising and worshipping God. The saints form, with the angels, a *host*, an army, who are ever near and waiting for us to call upon them, that they may come swiftly to our aid. As exorcist Fr. Athanasius said,

> The saints are our "big brothers" in the Faith who "made it." Their struggles were struggles with specific vices or challenges, and they now have a potency in that particular area to help us. Our Lord will assign a saint to a person in order to supply extra help for a certain struggle.[12]

The significance and efficacy that the Church attributes to recourse to the saints must awaken in us a renewed appreciation of their ability to assist us.

The Power of the Saints

The prayers of the Church proclaim the wonders of the saints throughout the liturgical year, especially on their feast days, when the Church asks God for specific forms of assistance through the intercession of the saints. In these prayers, we ask the saints to help us put away all deceits of error and be steadfast in faith, to defend us, to overcome the wiles of our enemies, to help us enjoy peace, to shield us from the snares of the devil, to defend us by their prayers, and to deliver us by their patronage from all adversities. Further still, according to the prayers of the Church, which God always hears and longs to answer, the saints help us to love God more fully, to believe in the help of Our Lady, to pray well, to turn away from the world, to long for Heaven, to find peace in this life, to be truly repentant, and to persevere in our journey to eternity.

---

[12] Fr. Athanasius, in discussion with Charles D. Fraune, July 2024.

In 1889, in an encyclical encouraging the faithful to increase their devotion to St. Joseph, Pope Leo XIII provided a clear and profound emphasis on the need to have recourse to the saints during our earthly pilgrimage:

During periods of stress and trial—chiefly when every lawlessness of act seems permitted to the powers of darkness—it has been the custom in the Church to plead with special fervor and perseverance to God, her author and protector, by recourse to the intercession of the saints—and chiefly of the Blessed Virgin, Mother of God—whose patronage has ever been the most efficacious. The fruit of these pious prayers and of the confidence reposed in the divine goodness, has always, sooner or later, been made apparent ... that God may be more favorable to our prayers, and that He may come with bounty and promptitude to the aid of His Church.[13]

An anecdote from the *Life of St. Alphonsus Liguori*, describing an incident shortly after his death in 1787, provides a classic example of the piety which we must form, and the "promptitude" with which the saints will answer, according to the will of God:

Doña Catherine Biscotti, a Benedictine nun of Salerno, after suffering for fourteen months from a grievous malady, was declared to be dying. The doctor thought mortification[14] had already set in. While in this state she exclaimed: "Alphonsus Liguori, prove to me that you are really a saint, as is everywhere proclaimed; you

---

[13] Pope Leo XIII, encyclical letter *Quamquam Pluries* (August 15, 1889), nos. 1–2.

[14] Seemingly, the "signs of death."

must cure me of this illness, and, as the process of your canonization will have to be drawn up, I promise to bear witness to my cure juridically, and to have a mass and a *Te Deum* sung in thanksgiving." Having said this, the nun fell asleep, and on awaking found that she was perfectly cured.[15]

The power of the saints is made manifest both during their lives and after their death. In their holy lives on earth, by the grace of God flowing through them, they raised the dead (St. Bernardine of Siena), healed the sick (St. Martin de Porres), drove out demons (St. Francis of Assisi), levitated (St. Joseph of Cupertino), read souls (St. John Vianney), bilocated (St. Alphonsus Liguori), bore the wounds of Christ in their bodies (St. Padre Pio), extinguished fires which were destroying cities (St. Florian), changed the weather (St. Peter Verona and St. Scholastica), calmed the elements of the earth (St. Vincent Ferrer), were immune to martyrdom (St. Cecilia and St. John the Apostle), and even "survived" death (St. Denis and many other "cephalophores"[16]).

By some special, divine inspiration, many saints also prophesied the power that they would possess after their death, stating to their followers that their spiritual power of intercession and miracles, greatly renowned as it was during their earthly lives, would be much greater once they entered Heaven. For example, just before he died, St. Dominic told his brethren, "Do not weep, my children; I shall be more useful to you where I am now going,

---

[15] *The Life of St. Alphonsus Liguori* (Charlotte, NC: Slaying Dragons Press, 2024), 499. "Juridically" here refers to making an official documentation of a purported miracle.

[16] A saint who, after having been decapitated, picked up his head and walked with it, often preaching at the same time.

than I have ever been in this life."[17] St. Catherine of Siena spoke similarly, as she lay dying, in order to comfort those surrounding her and mourning her death:

> Beloved sons, you ought not to be afflicted at my death; you should rather rejoice with me and congratulate me, because I am about to quit this land of exile, and repose in the unending peace of God. I give you the positive assurance that I shall be more useful to you after my decease, than I would, or could have been by remaining with you in this life so obscured by grief and so filled with miseries.[18]

Likewise, it is widely reported that St. Padre Pio told a follower: "I have made an agreement with the Lord—that when my soul is purified by the flames of purgatory and is worthy to enter heaven, I will stand at the gates of paradise and will not enter until I have seen the last of my sons and daughters enter."[19]

The saints had great power in life, and they have even greater power in Heaven. As Pope Pius XI recalled during his homily for her canonization Mass, St. Thérèse of Lisieux's dying promise was to spend her time in Heaven doing good on earth, in "letting fall upon earth a shower of Roses." And so, as the pope continued,

---

[17] Br. Raphael Forbing, O.P., "St. Dominic and the Ascension," *Dominicana*, May 23, 2012, www.dominicanajournal.org/st-dominic-and-the-ascension.

[18] Bl. Raymond of Capua, *The Life of St. Catherine of Sienna* (New York: P. J. Kenedy and Sons, 1862), 271.

[19] Sr. Bernadette Mary Reis, FSP, "Padre Pio: 'If Only I Could Help You to Help Others, Jesus,'" *Vatican News*, March 18, 2018, https://www.vaticannews.va/en/pope/news/2018-03/pope-francis-padre-piostigmata-confessor-healer.html.

"We desire earnestly that all the Faithful of Christ should render themselves worthy of partaking in the abundant profusion of graces resulting from the intercession of 'little Thérèse,'" and he reminded the faithful of "the innumerable wonders[20] wrought by Almighty God at her intercession." In the closing of his homily to the faithful, the Holy Father stated, "In our present needs, let us all invoke the patronage of St. Thérèse of the Child Jesus, that by her intercession, a shower of Roses, that is, of the graces we require, may descend upon us."[21] After all, she, and all the saints, are longing to help us.

The Litany of the Saints

As a result of the existence of this great company of heavenly patrons, which Scripture refers to as "so great a cloud of witnesses" (Heb. 12:1), the Church has, from her beginning, called upon the saints to aid the Church and all of her members as we do battle with the world, the flesh, and the devil. The saints are with us to encourage us, give us strength to persevere, help us let the old man of sin finally be laid to rest (see Col. 3:9), and ease our journey to Paradise, where we will join them in the eternal joys of Heaven.

As witness to this belief, the Church crafted what is known as the Litany of the Saints, an ancient prayer that calls upon a great number of the most notable saints in the history of the Church, asking them to intercede for us before God. This Litany

---

[20] He refers to this, in another place, as "a multitude of prodigies."

[21] Rev. Thomas N. Taylor, *Saint Thérèse of Lisieux, The Little Flower of Jesus* (New York: P. J. Kenedy and Sons, 1930), 271–274; available at www.ewtn.com/catholicism/library/canonization-13797.

has become a central spiritual component to many of the Church prayers and rituals. All three volumes of *The Roman Ritual*[22] contain a section for it, and it is part of many official blessings of the Church: of a baptismal font, of epiphany water, of a parish and its land, of a new church or oratory, of a cornerstone for a new church, of a new cemetery, of a school, of fields or mountain-meadows, and of a granary. It is also part of the ritual for many processions: on the Feast of St. Mark the Evangelist, the Corpus Christi procession, the many processions imploring God's help (for rain, fair weather, averting tempests, in time of famine, in time of epidemic or plague, in time of war, in time of tribulation), and, fittingly, in the procession for transferring the sacred relics of the saints.

The Litany of the Saints is the most ancient of all litanies that are still in use today, and it developed slowly, first focusing on the martyrs. A slightly different and shorter form than what we use today is mentioned by St. Basil in the fourth century and by others in the third century.[23] Over time, as more saints were

---

[22] *The Roman Ritual* is the Church's official book of sacred rites, including the sacraments and sacramental blessings such as exorcism. The quotations throughout this book are from *The Roman Ritual* promulgated in 1614, which, while still in use today, is often overshadowed by the modern *Book of Blessings* promulgated in 1984 as part of the liturgical reforms. The *Book of Blessings* takes a very different approach to sacramental blessings and very often lacks the richness and directness of the traditional *Ritual* as well as a proper connection to the history and traditional devotions of the Church. As a result, the traditional *Ritual* is preferred by many priests and scholars.

[23] This difference in length is probably because prior to the fourth century, only martyr-saints were publicly honored by the Church, since in the first centuries of the Church, the primary witness

declared, including non-martyrs, the Litany naturally expanded. Around the fourth century, when the vicious persecution of the Church ended, public processions and litanies became commonplace, and the faithful began reciting the Litany of the Saints, first on the Feast of St. Mark. As the years progressed, the Litany also became used for more events: it was joined to the Rogation days before the Ascension in 477,[24] and Pope St. Gregory the Great prescribed its recitation in 590 as part of a public procession in thanksgiving for the end of a terrible plague that had struck Rome.

The Power of the Litany in the Rite of Exorcism

The Litany of the Saints is a key component of the Rite of Exorcism. Fr. Amorth said, "For the one who is troubled by a demon, the invocation of the saints during the rite of exorcism manifests this trust of the Church in their presence."[25] The Rite of Exorcism therefore places this important prayer at the very beginning of its work of expelling the devil. Adam Blai, peritus of religious demonology and exorcism for the Diocese of Pittsburgh, Pennsylvania, remarked that the inclusion of the Litany of the Saints in the Rite of Exorcism is likely inspired

---

of fidelity to Christ involved death. Likewise, the Canon of the Mass, whose present form is due in large part to St. Gregory the Great, only mentions saints who were martyrs. See Msgr. John F. Sullivan, *The Externals of the Catholic Church: A Handbook of Catholic Usage* (New York: P. J. Kenedy and Sons, 1951), 360.

[24] Msgr. Sullivan, *The Externals of the Catholic Church*, 359. Rogation Days are days of prayer and fasting to appease God's anger, ask for His protection in calamities, and ask for a good harvest.

[25] Amorth, An *Exorcist Explains the Demonic*, 125.

by the fact that in the Church's history, the living saints[26] were very often the ones called upon to perform exorcisms.[27] We see this role especially in the life of St. Benedict, the patron saint of exorcists, who, despite not being ordained, once delivered a cleric from possession,[28] as well as in the life of St. Catherine of Siena, who exorcised a demon simply by tracing the sign of the cross on the possessed person's body.[29] Thus, the Church knew, as she constructed this rite, that the first thing to be done was to call upon the saints.

Exorcist Fr. John Szada, explaining the importance of having the Litany of the Saints as the first prayer in the rite, said, "That's why we start with the Litany of the Saints, because then you're calling on *all* of them."[30] Exorcist Fr. Athanasius declared, "I always start with the Litany of the Saints. I had an energumen[31] say that as soon as each saint is mentioned in the Litany, that saint is there, and he is eventually surrounded by saints."[32] Fr. Lampert agreed, adding:

> It's my experience that the saints show up during the Litany of the Saints, when the Church is calling upon these holy men and women to be present during this particular prayer of the Church, and to bring with them their own sanctity, their holiness, their virtue, all of those

---

26 I.e., those living Christians renowned for their holiness.

27 Adam Blai, *The History of Exorcism* (Manchester, NH: Sophia Institute Press, 2023), 91.

28 St. Gregory the Great, *The Life of St. Benedict: The Great Patriarch of the Western Monks* (Charlotte, NC: Tan Books, 2012), 32–33.

29 Bl. Raymond of Capua, *The Life of St. Catherine of Sienna*, 194.

30 Fr. John Szada, in discussion with Patrick O'Hearn, August 2024.

31 A possessed person.

32 Fr. Athanasius, in discussion with Charles D. Fraune, July 2024.

elements that allow them to become a part of the Communion of Saints.[33]

Dave VanVickle, a Catholic layman who has assisted exorcists for many years and who travels widely teaching on the topic of spiritual warfare, gave a wonderful explanation as to why the Litany of the Saints is so powerful in exorcism:

> One of the reasons that the exorcism ritual starts with the Litany of Saints is not just to ask for prayer. It's to say to the demon, "Look, *this* is the Church we represent. *This* person beat you, and *this* person beat you, and *this* person beat you, and you have no hope of any possible victory today, because *this* is who you're up against." It's not just the faith of the priest, or the faith of people praying, or the strength of the demon. [The demon is coming against] the eternal, infinite power of God played out in the history of the Church, and we remind him, "Look, you're beaten already, and all these guys are reminders of how you've been beaten."[34]

Indeed, throughout the Rite of Exorcism, the Church continuously reminds the demon of all that God has done to conquer him and of the power of Christ that frustrates and crushes his plans. It holds up, through the words of the priest, all of the signs of Christ's victory, reminding the demon that these have

---

[33] Fr. Vincent Lampert, in discussion with Patrick O'Hearn, August 2024.

[34] B. T. Wallace, host, *Truth and Shadow Podcast*, episode 25, "Rising Darkness: The Resurgence of Exorcism," featuring Dave VanVickle, YouTube, April 18, 2024, https://youtu.be/boSeVTuKYqg?si =n4P99RPC8PoPXqQB.

vanquished him and he must now give way and depart. As Fr. Lampert explained,

> In an exorcism, what the Church is doing is throwing into the face of the demons the elements of the Christian Faith that the demons themselves have rejected. So they've rejected the Truth and you can say the saints bring with them the Truth of our Faith. Since they bring that Truth, and because the demons have rejected it, that's why these saints are so powerful in helping to expel demons.[35]

Some exorcists also take the liberty of adding additional saints to the Litany, inserting the ones whose help they would like on that particular occasion. Fr. Pius said,

> Part of my own personal technique was to have a lengthy Litany of the Saints and to see how the demoniac reacted to different saints in this Litany. That would often guide how we would then unfold the rest of the prayer time together. That was very often in conjunction with particular memorials or feasts that were happening liturgically.[36]

Similarly, Fr. Pius added:

> When the demoniac is reacting against this or that saint, I would then invoke that saint repeatedly. So it's an art, it's not a science, and the art of the Rite of Exorcism is obviously marching through a long series of prayers, formulaic prayers, but it's also interjecting, with some charismatic[37]

---

[35] Fr. Vincent Lampert, in discussion with Patrick O'Hearn, August 2024.

[36] Fr. Pius, in discussion with Patrick O'Hearn, September 2024.

[37] I.e., an inspired prayer.

kind of prayer, and also some accommodation of those prayers, like the Litany of the Saints.[38]

Fr. Lampert said that, as the priest prays through the rite, he makes mental notes of the parts of the rite which have a more profound impact on the demon, including the Litany of the Saints and the specific saints that are mentioned. "If the demons react more strongly to a particular saint, then you really reinforce invoking that saint," Father stated.[39] Fr. Timothy said, "Our team in exorcisms will watch carefully to see which saints especially cause the demon to flip out. When they notice something, I'll stop and go back and repeat over and over again that particular name."[40]

Adam Blai, in his book *The Exorcism Files*, shared many stories highlighting the power of the Litany of the Saints. In many of the reported cases, Blai stated that it was during the Litany of the Saints that the demons began to react, even when it was simply Blai, a layman, who was pronouncing the prayer. It is not always the case that the demon departs during the Litany, but it has happened on a few occasions.

One such case involved a woman named Molly, who, after deepening her New Age practices, had become convinced that she was being oppressed, in disturbing ways, by what appeared to be a demon.[41] At her request, Adam went to see her to offer his

---

[38] Fr. Pius, in discussion with Patrick O'Hearn, September 2024.

[39] Ibid.

[40] Fr. Timothy, in discussion with Charles D. Fraune, August 2024. Exorcists today typically work with a team, whose support is often critical, especially when taking note of how the demon is reacting to the various elements of the Rite.

[41] "*Oppression* is when demonic spirits trouble a person, can speak in their mind, physically hurt them, and affect their body in various other ways" (Blai, *The History of Exorcism*, 12), whereas *possession*

help and pray the Litany of the Saints. As he recounted, "After the second time through the Litany, whatever was oppressing Molly broke and left. She suddenly had peace and quiet in her mind for the first time in months. She immediately said she was going to learn all she could about Jesus and dedicate her life to thanking Him for saving her."[42]

In another case, Adam was sent to speak to a woman who had become greatly disturbed as a result of her and her husband's involvement in ghost-hunting. Her symptoms included, among other things, hearing a persistent voice that she could not control. "I simply prayed the Litany of the Saints, as I always did for spiritual problems," Blai said. He continued:

> About halfway through the Litany, the wife let out a sudden cry and threw her arms around her husband. She was sobbing loudly and clutching him tightly. She said over and over that she was sorry, and she kissed his cheek and hugged him while he sobbed as well. I asked her if she still heard the voice, and she said no. Her expressions returned and she seemed clear in her thinking and speech. I finished the Litany to be sure, then packed up.[43]

The Litany of the Saints is an especially powerful tool against the forces of evil because it calls upon all of the saints to pray for us and reminds demons of their many failures and shortcomings. We must always remember that the power of the saints is a clear, ancient, and enduring reality in the life of the Church, solemnly

---

entails a state in which the demon takes over the person's body to a certain extent.

[42] Adam Blai, *The Exorcism Files: True Stories of Demonic Possession* (Manchester, NH: Sophia Institute Press, 2022), 60.

[43] Ibid., 106–107.

taught as a divinely revealed truth and actually witnessed in the earthly and heavenly lives of these holy men and women. Through the divinely established Communion of Saints, our victorious brethren are able to share with us the riches of grace and glory which they now enjoy in Heaven. And so the Church does not hesitate to call upon *all of them* as often as she can, and she desires that her faithful children follow her example.

2

Merit and Authority in
the Kingdom of God

The Church's tradition of entrusting herself and her earthly members to the protection and intercession of the saints in Heaven goes back to at least the fourth century, when local Churches began to take the martyrs as their patrons as the Church finally emerged from beneath the shroud of incessant persecution. Yet the quick spread of this practice implies that this belief was part of the Church's theology well before this time.

The ability of the saints to assist us from Heaven is tied to many theological realities: our union with Christ through grace, our conformity with Him through Baptism, our share in His work of redemption through our participation in His divine life, the divine promise of rewards for the good deeds we do in this life, and our participation in Christ's heavenly reign after death (see 2 Tim. 2:11–12). As Pope Pius XII taught in 1943, Christians "cooperate with Him in dispensing the graces of Redemption"[44] and "in this work of salvation,"[45] "a cooperation which they must

---

[44] Pope Pius XII, encyclical letter *Mystici Corporis Christi* (June 29, 1943), no. 12.

[45] Ibid., no. 59.

offer to our Divine Savior as though they were His associates."[46] On earth, this cooperation in the work of Redemption is like a seed, only planted; it achieves its full flowering and fruitfulness in Heaven. *Lumen Gentium,* the Dogmatic Constitution on the Church, explained:

> For by reason of the fact that those in heaven are more closely united with Christ, they establish the whole Church more firmly in holiness, lend nobility to the worship which the Church offers to God here on earth and in many ways contribute to its greater edification. For after they have been received into their heavenly home and are present to the Lord, through Him and with Him and in Him, they do not cease to intercede with the Father for us, showing forth the merits which they won on earth through the one Mediator between God and man.... Thus by their brotherly interest our weakness is greatly strengthened.[47]

And so the saints never leave us; they continue, through their prayers, to help us work out our salvation, and they offer their powers as the Church Triumphant to those still fighting as the Church Militant.

To Reign with Christ

In 1927, Pope Pius XI wrote that man has been set upon this earth that he may "attain the sublime end for which he was

---

[46] Ibid., no. 44.

[47] Vatican Council II, Dogmatic Constitution on the Church *Lumen Gentium* (November 21, 1964), no. 49.

created."[48] We see a glimpse of how great this end is by reflecting on what St. Athanasius wrote around the year 360 in *The Life of St. Anthony* (also known as *St. Antony of the Desert*) regarding the envy that the demons have for mankind: "The demons were not made as demons, for God made nothing bad. But they also were created beautiful, but fell from heavenly wisdom.... They envy us Christians and move everything to hinder us from the way to Heaven, lest we mount to where they fell from."[49] This truth, that man is destined for the eternal glory that the demons lost and do not want us to attain, is too little known and is seldom preached about today, though it is perpetually on the lips, and at the tips of the pens, of the great saints and Doctors of the Church: man is created to reign with Christ in Heaven and will be seated in his position, to varying degrees, among the choirs of angels, according to the reward due to him according to his good deeds.

St. Thomas Aquinas spoke about these varying degrees of glory and beatitude: "According to those who maintain that the chief devil was of the highest order, it is probable that some fell of every order; just as men are taken up into every order to supply for the angelic ruin."[50] The angelic ruin led to the abandoning of heavenly "thrones," that is, places of dignity and governance and holiness that were first entrusted to the spirits whom God created in the nine choirs, and the elect, the men and women who conform their lives to the will of God and obtain their salvation, will fill these thrones when they "reign with Christ" in the Kingdom of Heaven

---

[48] Pope Pius XI, encyclical letter *Divini Illius Magistri* (December 31, 1929), no. 7.

[49] St. Athanasius, *St. Antony of the Desert*, trans. Dom J. B. McLaughlin, O.S.B. (Charlotte, NC: Tan Books, 2014), 29–30.

[50] St. Thomas Aquinas, *Summa Theologica* I, q. 63, art. 9.

(see 2 Tim. 2:11–12). For, as *Lumen Gentium* adds, "before we reign with Christ in glory, all of us will be made manifest 'before the tribunal of Christ, so that each one may receive what he has won through the body, according to his works.'"[51]

St. Thomas Aquinas referred to this "reign" as "equality with the angels," stating, "Equality with the angels is promised to the saints … since man's soul and an angel are ordained alike for beatitude."[52] The modern *Catechism* states that the Blessed in the Church in Heaven "are also, to various degrees, associated with the holy angels in the divine governance exercised by Christ in glory" (CCC 1053).[53] *Lumen Gentium* added that those who behold God as He is do so "in various ways and degrees," all the while being "in communion in the same charity of God and neighbor."[54] This doctrine was also proclaimed by the Council of Florence[55] and the Council of Trent.[56]

The saints in Heaven, though they do not yet experience the glory that will manifest in their risen bodies, nonetheless understand in their souls the full glory of God and of their

---

[51] *Lumen Gentium*, no. 48.

[52] St. Thomas Aquinas, *Summa Theologica* I, q. 62, art. 5. "Beatitude" here means living in union with God in eternity.

[53] See also Pope St. Paul VI, *Solemni Hac Liturgia* (Credo of the People of God) (June 30, 1968), no. 29; *Lumen Gentium*, no. 49.

[54] *Lumen Gentium*, no. 49.

[55] The Council of Florence declared that in Heaven, the souls of the perfectly just "clearly behold the Triune and One God as He is, but corresponding to the difference of their merits, the one more perfectly than the other" (Ludwig Ott, *Fundamentals of Catholic Dogma* (Rockford, IL: TAN Books, 1974), 479).

[56] The Council of Trent defined that the justified person merits an increase of the heavenly glory by good works (Council of Trent, Session 6, "On Justification," January 13, 1547, can. 32).

own salvation and glorification, "what he has won through the body, according to his works."[57] What St. Paul once exclaimed, they now know: "For I reckon that the sufferings of this time are not worthy to be compared with the glory to come, that shall be revealed in us" (Rom. 8:18, Douay-Rheims). Those who believe now, that is, the Church on earth, behold by faith His glory in His saints and know the goodness that He bestows upon us, even this very day, through their intercession, and we look forward to the Day of Judgment, when Christ will "be glorified in His saints" and will "be marveled at in all who have believed" (2 Thess. 1:10).

What Specific Saints Have Merited

The holiness we merit by prayer and cooperation with Christ in His work of redemption adds to the glory of God and brings many souls with us into Paradise. The saints therefore rightly dedicated their lives to obedience to Christ, seeking the reward that He had promised to those who "lay up for yourselves treasures in Heaven" (Matt. 6:20). The Blessed Mother herself, dear to all the saints, encourages us to keep this reward in mind, and she promises to those who faithfully pray the Rosary: "The faithful children of the Rosary shall merit a high degree of glory in heaven."[58]

As many saints have borne witness, and as St. Alphonsus teaches, this life "is not a place of rest, but of labors and sufferings; and it is for this end that God makes us live here." This is good and true because "it is by patience that we gain heaven.

---

[57] *Lumen Gentium*, no. 48.

[58] One of the fifteen promises of the Rosary, as revealed to St. Dominic and Bl. Alan de la Roche.

This earth is a place where we can gain merit; [and] by patience we may obtain the glory of paradise."[59] Times of trial, suffering, and temptation are permitted by God "for our advantage," to try our patience "that He may enrich us with greater merits and the goods of heaven,"[60] since these sufferings force us to unite ourselves more closely to Him, redouble our prayers, "and thereby acquire greater merits for heaven."[61] Therefore, at times, the greater the sufferings a saint experienced during life, the greater power his or her intercession may have from Heaven.

Fr. Athanasius highlighted St. Bruno as a good example of how a saint can merit, from the holiness of his earthly life, a specific heavenly role, especially through his work against the diabolical:

> There is a pond near where he is buried. It was St. Bruno's practice to go in there as a penitential exercise, up to his neck in the icy cold water. Up until recent times, the possessed would go into this pond, on the grounds of the Carthusian monastery,[62] to be delivered from the demon. The energumen who came to visit the pond were so loud that the monastery eventually restricted access to the pond! Carthusians are a semi-eremitic order. The constant screaming day and night made their lifestyle impossible.[63]

---

[59] St. Alphonsus Liguori, *A Christian's Rule of Life (with Darts of Fire)* (Charlotte, NC: Slaying Dragons Press), 67.

[60] Ibid., 69–70.

[61] Ibid., 70–71.

[62] Serra San Bruno, in Calabria, where St. Bruno is buried.

[63] Fr. Athanasius, in discussion with Charles D. Fraune, July 2024. Access to the pond seems to have been restricted sometime in the 1970s.

Fr. Athanasius explained that this pond functions like a third-class relic, something touched by the saint that can bring tangible spiritual benefits.

In one of his books, Fr. Amorth provides a liturgical prayer in honor of St. Antonino, a sixth-century miracle-worker monk who was once blessed with a vision of St. Michael the Archangel. In this prayer, we see how the Church connects the life of an individual saint with that saint's particular power to intercede for us. The prayer presents the fact that St. Antonino possessed "a special power against the devils" and, as a result of that gift, the Church asks Our Lord that, "through his merits and prayers, we may be liberated from their pitfalls and thus reach eternal life."[64]

God has granted specific rewards, merits, and authority to certain saints, and so the Church has established specific saints as the patrons of specific causes. This patronage is tied to the spiritual gifts, heroic virtues, battles against sin and Satan, forms of suffering, and evangelical achievements that have come to characterize the individual saint. Thus, St. Teresa of Ávila, who suffered from headaches, is the patron saint of those who suffer from headaches, as well as the patroness of Spain, the country in which she lived. St. Matthew, the Apostle, previously a tax collector, is the patron of accountants, bookkeepers, and, yes, tax collectors. St. John Bosco, who published books and pamphlets for spreading the Faith, is the patron of editors and publishers. St. Elizabeth Ann Seton, who worked to educate children and establish parochial schools, is the patron of Catholic schools. St. Dymphna, who

---

[64] Fr. Gabriele Amorth and Marcello Stanzione, *The Devil Is Afraid of Me: The Life and Work of the World's Most Famous Exorcist*, trans. Charlotte J. Fasi (Manchester, NH: Sophia Institute Press, 2019), 136.

died at the hands of her father, the king, after excessive grief led to his mental collapse, is the patron saint of those suffering from nervous or mental afflictions.

A 1927 declaration of Pope Pius XI explains further why the Church declares a saint to be the "patron" of a certain cause. Speaking of St. Thérèse of Lisieux, who was known for her great but insatiable missionary desires and for her promise to rain down roses (graces) from Heaven after her death, the declaration stated, "even among those scattered regions of the unfaithful, the Virgin of Carmel has not neglected to send down her promised shower of roses from Heaven"; indeed, "all have known [her] miraculous deeds [even] in pagan lands." The decree continues, "For this reason, innumerable bishops have thoroughly deemed that great fruits can be gained in the Lord's vineyard if St. Teresa of the Infant Jesus, who was burning with the greatest ardor and zeal for the Faith that must be extended ... is declared the heavenly patroness of all missionaries working in any mission." These bishops "most humbly offered their collected prayers from every place to our Most Holy Lord Pope Pius XI," and so St. Teresa was named "the special patron of all missionaries, whether male or female, and also the patron of existing missions in the whole world, equally first with St. Francis Xavier."[65]

As an additional example of the specific powers of saints, Fr. Athanasius spoke of the intercessory power of St. Dominic Savio, the patron of youth and delinquents, stating, "He is one who never sinned mortally but was terribly tempted in his life.

---

[65] Pope Pius XI, Decree *Apostolicorum in Missionibus* (December 14, 1927), Papal Encyclicals, https://www.papalencyclicals.net /pius11/p11apost.htm. (Translated from the Latin by Laura Bement.)

This temptation, and his fidelity to purity, made him 'a living martyr,' as St. John Bosco said, and now he is a great intercessor for purity and for the youth."[66] Father's description reminds us of St. Alphonsus's reasoning that God often gives us a unique opportunity by permitting us to face grueling temptations, since by uniting ourselves more closely to Christ and redoubling our prayers, we "acquire greater merits for Heaven."

Pope St. John Paul II is widely known as a powerful aid to exorcists in their ministry. Fr. Amorth described why the saintly pope has come to merit such intercessory power:

> I have asked the demon[67] more than once, "Why are you so scared of John Paul II?" and I have had two different responses, both interesting. One, "because he disrupted my plans." And I think that he is referring to the fall of communism in Russia and Eastern Europe. The collapse of communism. Another response that he gave me: "because he pulled so many young people from my hands." There are so many young people who, thanks to John Paul II, were converted. Perhaps some were already Christian but not practicing, but

---

[66] Fr. Athanasius, in discussion with Charles D. Fraune, July 2024.

[67] While the exorcist is always skeptical and dismissive of what a demon might reveal, sometimes a demon will tell the truth. Many exorcists ignore everything said by a demon that does not directly pertain to the case of possession at hand. However, there are times when a further interrogation is warranted for the sake of the soul involved, which occasionally provokes the demon to admit the truth about something that is beneficial to the faithful. While the demon may indeed utter something true, despite being, by nature, a liar, we are forbidden to turn to him for theological insights. We must never cross the line and make the demon a source of theological truths.

then with John Paul II they came back to the practice. "He pulled so many young people out of my hands."[68]

The virtues and good works of these saints, and their ability to withstand suffering and overcome temptation, therefore carry over into their heavenly lives and merit for them unique intercessory gifts so that they may come to our aid in special circumstances.

Meriting a Triumph over Satan

After death, the specific holiness of each of the saints and the merits (rewards) they have received for their good deeds establishes them in the Kingdom of Heaven in certain positions of spiritual authority. This authority is then exercised in and through Christ for our benefit, including, among many other miracles, assistance in our battle against the minions of Satan.

The connection between holiness and the power to drive out the devil has been clear since the start of Christianity. Principally, it is in Christ's own Person, in whom holiness dwelt in its fullness, that we see the ultimate power over Satan. Then, in the lives of His faithful followers, this power is shared. Our Lord entrusted an authority over demons to His Apostles, but He extended this power to include "those who believe" (Mark 16:17). Further, He specified that some demons will not be driven out except through "prayer and fasting" (Mark 9:29), two of the primary means of spiritual growth and holiness that are accessible to all Christians, not simply the ordained.

---

[68] "Rome's Exorcist Finding John Paul II Effective against Satan," Catholic News Agency, May 17, 2011, https://www.catholic newsagency.com/news/22558/romes-exorcist-finding-john-paul -ii-effective-against-satan.

In the early Church, unlike today, there was not yet a rule tying the work of exorcism exclusively to the priesthood. As a result, there were a great many saints, from all states of life (ordained, religious, and lay), who were gifted with the power to drive out demons. These "charismatic exorcisms" were typically done by Christians who were "very prayerful, devout, ascetic, chaste, and often graced with other mystical experiences and phenomena."[69] These exorcisms were not formal rites of the Church but were usually "*ad hoc* exorcisms created in the moment."[70] Stories of such exorcisms grew in popularity beginning in the fourth century, as they encouraged Christians to be more devoted to the saints.

The power behind these exorcisms seemed to lay in the holiness of the saint, and the ability to perform exorcisms was seen as strong evidence for a person's sanctity. Fr. Amorth highlighted that this same holiness is also necessary for the priest in official exorcisms today. Exorcisms do not function like the sacraments, which bring the supernatural effect *ex opere operato*, that is, simply by the fact that the priest prayed the rite properly, regardless of his holiness. Instead, exorcisms function like all sacramentals, bringing the supernatural effect *ex opere operantis*, that is, they are impacted also by the piety of the priest or of the person using the sacramental. Thus, "the more faith an exorcist brings to the table," Fr. Amorth said, "the more effective he will be. This is why the mere presence of some saints has been enough to drive out demons."[71] In the end, the best exorcist would be a saint too.

---

[69] Blai, *The History of Exorcism*, 67.

[70] Ibid., 65.

[71] The editors of Sophia Institute Press, *The Pope's Exorcist: 101 Questions about Fr. Gabriele Amorth* (Manchester, NH: Sophia Institute Press, 2022), 71–72.

Saints in the Rite of Exorcism

Within the Rite of Exorcism itself, we see that the Church, in her official prayers, is very much aware of the intercessory power of the saints. Early on in the rite, after the Litany of the Saints, many readings from the Gospels, and a few prayers, the priest begins the *commands* against the demon. It is here that we note an important involvement of the saints. The priest commands the demons to leave, clarifying that it is not just because the priest is saying so, but because "it is God Himself who commands thee!"[72] The priest repeats this command, invoking each Person of the Blessed Trinity as the One who commands the demon to depart. Further, he adds, "The mystery of the Cross commands thee!"[73] Immediately after this, the saints are called upon, though only Sts. Peter and Paul are specifically named: "The faith of the holy apostles Peter and Paul and the other saints commands thee! The blood of the martyrs commands thee! The constancy of the confessors commands thee! The devout intercession of all holy men and women commands thee!"[74]

After the Rite of Exorcism, the Church provides another prayer for priests to use that is intended to drive demons out of locations rather than persons. This is called "Exorcism against Satan and the Fallen Angels." Within this prayer, the priest says, "We cast thee out," invoking wording nearly identical to the rite itself. At the end of this prayer, as above when the saints are invoked, the priest says,

> The most excellent Virgin Mary, Mother of God commands thee, who in her lowliness crushed thy proud head

---

[72] *The Roman Ritual*, vol. 2, *Christian Burial, Exorcisms, Reserved Blessings, Etc.* (Caritas Publishing, 2017), 189.

[73] Ibid.

[74] Ibid.

from the first moment of her Immaculate Conception! The faith of the holy apostles Peter and Paul and the other apostles commands thee! The blood of the martyrs commands thee, as well as the pious intercession of holy men and women!

Within the commands of this prayer, we are also taught why Sts. Peter and Paul are particularly effective against the devil, as if in answer to the devil's protestation of the fact. The priest asks the demon the rhetorical question, "But why dost thou linger here yet longer?" just before he proceeds to answer with the following command:

Give place to the Holy Spirit, who, through His holy apostle, Peter, struck thee down openly in Simon … who smote thee with the night of blindness in Elymas, the magician, at the word of thine apostle, Paul, and at his command bade thee likewise to go out of Pythonissa, the soothsayer.[75]

This final prayer also contains an invocation very similar to the *Confiteor* of Holy Mass, in which the priest and the people confess their sins in the presence of the Communion of Saints, stating (in the extraordinary form), "I confess to Almighty God, to Blessed Mary ever Virgin, to Blessed Michael the Archangel, to Blessed John the Baptist, to the Holy Apostles Peter and Paul, and to all the saints." The exorcism prayer likewise states:

In the Name of Jesus Christ, our Lord and God, with confidence in the intercession of the Virgin Mary, Mother of God, of Blessed Michael the Archangel, of the holy

---

[75] *The Roman Ritual*, vol. 2, 195. See Acts 8, 13, and 16.

apostles Peter and Paul, and all the saints, and with assurance in the sacred power of our ministry, we steadfastly proceed with the task of expelling the molestations of the devil's frauds.[76]

The saints abundantly demonstrate that when we bind ourselves to Christ, His divine power can flow freely through us and into our world. These saints are invaluable aids, seasoned warriors who stand at the ready to surround us and go before us in battle. Fortified with this knowledge and with the power of these allies, we are incorporated into Christ's work of redemption by the generous love of God. Let us heed the example of exorcists, whose ministry depends upon the intercession of the Church Triumphant, upon those who have been victorious over the evil one, and let us realize that our own efforts to persevere in grace also depend on the help of our victorious brethren.

[76] *The Roman Ritual*, vol. 2, 225. NB: the prayers within the rite itself do not mention Our Lady, though the rite recommends invoking her after the specific prayers have concluded. The rite also provides the Athanasian Creed and many Psalms as extra prayers to utilize, saying of the Our Father, the Hail Mary, and the Creed, "it will be very helpful to say [these] devoutly over and over again" (*The Roman Ritual*, vol. 2, 195). It also recommends saying the Magnificat at this point.

3

The Saints Wield Their Power Against Demons

We know that the saints have remarkable power over evil because demons will not even speak their names. Indeed, within an exorcism, demons often use indirect language when referring to the various supernatural powers that are working against them. Fr. Amorth explained that normally, "It can happen that demons will make a reference to God, to the Virgin, and to some saints, although they have an authentic terror of them, but it never happens that they are able to use their names directly."[77]

Fr. Amorth continued:

> If they must mention them, they use substitutions. Jesus is referred to in reference to the priest who is performing the exorcism, such as, "your leader" or "your superior"; our Lady is "that one there" or "the thief of souls"; the saints are "assassins." They oppose [the saints] because, by their prayers, [the saints] steal souls from [the demons'] claws.[78]

---

[77] Amorth, *An Exorcist Explains the Demonic*, 126–127.
[78] Ibid., 127.

This manner of speech reveals something important. The name of God and the names of His saints are powerful, as the *Catechism* states: "A name expresses a person's essence and identity and the meaning of this person's life.... To disclose one's name is to make oneself known to others" (CCC 203). Thus, even the saint's *name* strikes terror in a demon. Fr. Girolamo Menghi, a sixteenth-century priest who is often called "The Father of the Exorcist's Art," even said that one of many signs by which an exorcist can determine whether a demon is truly present within a person's body is "if he witnesses the hands of the subject tremble ... or when they make sudden or unusual movements or spasms, or show pain and repulsion, at the mention of ... the names of saints."[79]

The reason that even the very name of a saint is so powerful is because saints are the citizens of Heaven, and the demons are fully aware that they themselves lost such a citizenship by an act of their own free will. "So the demons see these saints," Fr. Lampert explained, "as those who are where they once were, but they turned away. There is an agitation that comes from that."[80] This agitation is so effective in ending the activity of a demon in the life of an individual that exorcisms have long invoked the saints as a central aspect of the process of liberation. As we read from an ancient rite of exorcism: "May all the power of the devil be extinguished in you, N., through the imposition of our hands or, rather, through the invocation of the holy archangels, angels,

---

[79] Fr. Girolamo Menghi, O.F.M., *The Scourge of Demons*, trans. Fr. Robert Nixon, O.S.B. (Charlotte, NC: Slaying Dragons Press, 2025), 14.

[80] Fr. Vincent Lampert, in discussion with Patrick O'Hearn, August 2024.

patriarchs, prophets, apostles, martyrs, confessors, virgins, and all the saints together. Amen."[81] The exorcists therefore realize that they are constantly acting with the saints in their ministry, as revealed in another prayer: "I bind and enchain you, just as the saints of God did bind and constrain demons."[82]

Fr. Lampert provided a wonderful way of understanding what is happening when a saint begins to oppose a demon in an exorcism. He said:

> It's almost like that particular saint (think of that halo around their head) is radiating that virtue of God, and it almost becomes blinding to the demons. They're lashing out in anger and despair. This is due to the fact that during the Rite of Exorcism, after the priest prays through the rite once completely, as he is required to do, he then goes back and repeats those particular parts, and those particular saints, which caused a strong reaction in the demon. Then the demon will cry out, "Why is that one here?" or "Make that one go away!" It's almost like they want that light to go out so that the darkness can remain.[83]

Like beacons of supernatural light, the saints blind and confuse the demons when they come to the assistance of the faithful. Exorcists see the power of the saints play out in concrete ways, from terrorizing the demons by the mere sound of their names to standing in opposition to specific demons, becoming what exorcists call a "nemesis."

---

[81] Menghi, *The Scourge of Demons*, 85.
[82] Ibid.
[83] Fr. Vincent Lampert, in discussion with Patrick O'Hearn, August 2024.

The Nemesis

The powerful role granted to the saints in the work against sin and Satan establishes them, in varying degrees and in varying roles, as permanent citadels of supernatural assistance on the enduring battlefield of salvation. These saints in these positions of power have become known, at least in modern times, by the name of "nemesis," for they have become the archenemies of particular members of the kingdom of Satan.[84] As Fr. Ripperger said, "Every demon has a nemesis."[85]

Fr. Menghi's classic book on exorcisms, *Flagellum Daemonum*, "The Scourge of Demons," supports the idea that certain saints serve as the nemeses to certain demons. Fr. Menghi counseled within a sixteenth-century Rite of Exorcism that the exorcist should question the demon(s) regarding "who are its particular

---

[84] Though the positioning of a specific saint against a specific demon may sound similar to the Manichaen positioning of a "light force" against a "dark force," this Christian reality is entirely different. Manichaeanism posits a struggle between an eternal good and an eternal evil, rejecting the belief that the One True God is supreme over all things. The Christian concept of a nemesis is merely one way the spiritual battle plays out in time among creatures, as seen with St. Michael, a specific archangel, who was given a concrete role against Satan, a specific demon. In addition, it can be seen in the way that specific virtues oppose specific vices, in which the saints who master a certain virtue would then be particularly in opposition to a demon who mastered a certain vice. Further, this reality has been observed in the history of the Church, as noted in Fr. Menghi's sixteenth-century classic manual, *The Scourge of Demons*, which presents this as a reality and bears the imprimatur of the Church.

[85] Fr. Chad Ripperger, "Our Lady of Sorrows and Healing," March 12, 2023, by Sensus Fidelium, YouTube, https://www.youtube .com/watch?v=QqKV28eSaWo.

foes, both in Heaven (among the saints and angels) and also in Hell (among its fellow demons)."[86] In addition, the exorcist must question the demon about "which saint it fears most strongly; [and] whom it regards as its greatest or particular foes, both among the angels and saints in Heaven and the demons in Hell."[87] Further, Fr. Menghi said that among the pertinent and permissible questions the exorcist may ask the demon(s) is "through which person or by which saint they are able to be expelled most readily."[88]

Fr. Lampert explained that the nemesis relationship between saints and demons is quite natural because:

> Demons may be associated with a particular vice, one of the deadly sins, but the saints are associated with a particular virtue. So when you have that virtue encountering the vice, in a particular case, then you get that big reaction, and then you come to know which particular saint can be a powerful ally to the exorcist in that case.[89]

Therefore, just as the vice of avarice is countered by the virtue of generosity, or the vice of lust is countered by the virtue of chastity, the saints in their virtue oppose the demons in their respective vices. Alternatively, the saint may have particular power over a certain demon because that saint overcame a specific vice while he or she was alive. "That's where the nemesis relationship exists," Fr. Szada explained, "because these saints were able to overcome these particular demons while they were here on earth."[90] The lives and

---

[86] Menghi, *The Scourge of Demons*, 61.

[87] Ibid., 60.

[88] Ibid., 18.

[89] Fr. Vincent Lampert, in discussion with Patrick O'Hearn, August 2024.

[90] Fr. John Szada, in discussion with Patrick O'Hearn, August 2024.

writings of the Fathers of the Church and the Desert Fathers, such as St. Athanasius, who heroically endured unending diabolical assaults, and St. Benedict, whose power over the devil led to the creation of the famous St. Benedict medal, are an especially great source of learning about how saints gained a particular power over the devil as a result of faithfully enduring Satan's incessant attacks.

One saint we can always invoke in our fight against evil is St. Paul. Though research for this book did not uncover evidence of St. Paul assisting exorcists from Heaven, or being the nemesis of a particular demon, it is probable that he is, based on his account in his Second Letter to the Corinthians, in which he said, "And to keep me from being too elated by the abundance of revelations, a thorn was given me in the flesh, a messenger of Satan, to harass me, to keep me from being too elated" (2 Cor. 12:7). As St. Paul went on to explain, he begged Our Lord three times to take away this demon. However, Our Lord had permitted it for a reason, as He replied, "My grace is sufficient for you, for my power is made perfect in weakness" (2 Cor. 12:8–9). While the details of this nemesis-style relationship are unclear, the fact that a specific demon was here assigned to oppose a specific saint mirrors the reality of the nemesis connection.

St. Padre Pio was also permitted to be assaulted by the demons perpetually. This, as Fr. Lampert explained, "was a gift from God." He continued, "God was permitting him to be afflicted because in the battles that St. Padre Pio encountered with the devil, he gained knowledge about the devil. Then he used that knowledge with people that he ministered to, who came to him, who were being afflicted by the evil one."[91] We can then imagine that whatever

---

[91] Fr. Vincent Lampert, in discussion with Patrick O'Hearn, August 2024.

imperfect knowledge Padre Pio was able to gain during life was then perfected in Heaven, meaning that his aid against evil is even more powerful now than it was during his earthly life.

In his talks, Fr. Ripperger has named a few of the saints whose specific nemesis relationship has become clearer. First, he said, "Our Lady, under the title of Immaculate Conception, is the nemesis of Satan; under the title of Seat of Wisdom, she's the nemesis of Lucifer; under the title of the Immaculate Heart, she's the nemesis of Baal."[92] Other saints who serve as nemeses against Satan include St. Catherine of Siena[93] and St. Rita of Cascia,[94] though Fr. Ripperger admitted that their specific nemeses remain indiscernible.

Some nemesis relationships pivot around demons or events in Sacred Scripture. The "noonday devil," a demon named in the Psalms (90:6 Douay-Rheims)[95] and mentioned by the Desert Fathers, refers to the temptation toward acedia, or spiritual sloth, which often attacks our perseverance at midday. The nemesis to this demon seems to be St. Catherine of Alexandria.[96] Another nemesis with a tie to Sacred Scripture is the archangel St. Raphael, the nemesis to the demon Asmodeus, with whom he battles in

---

[92] Fr. Chad Ripperger, "Our Lady of Sorrows and Healing." Some exorcists comment that these three names for the devil reflect a punishment from God in the form of a trifurcation of the devil's personality.

[93] Fr. Chad Ripperger, "Fr. Ripperger's Widest Range of Topics in One Show," September 18, 2024, by Spiritual Strength with Gene Zannetti, YouTube, https://www.youtube.com/watch?v=gEKdA4xx6io.

[94] Ibid.

[95] Psalm 91:6 RSVCE.

[96] Fr. Chad Ripperger, "Our Lady of Sorrows and Healing."

the Book of Tobit.[97] Finally, St. Matthias is the nemesis, as Fr. Ripperger put it, of "the spirit that claims to be Judas."[98]

Fr. Ripperger also provided a fascinating story that connects St. Joan of Arc to a demon discerned to have been conquered by her in this nemesis relationship. As Father stated, one demon, who presented itself under a title similar to one assigned to Satan in the Rite of Exorcism, that of "inciter of treason" and specifically "treason through ambition," said his nemesis was St. Joan of Arc. Father discussed this connection:

> What's interesting is that she became the nemesis of Satan precisely because the bishop that persecuted her and put her to death was doing so because he was ambitious. He was committing treason against France [and] was trying to move up in the ecclesiastical ranks because he wanted a different bishopric.[99]

Father continued to explain that during the rehabilitation trials of St. Joan of Arc, she responded, when asked what the one thing

[97] Fr. Chad Ripperger, "Fr. Ripperger's Widest Range of Topics in One Show."

[98] Ibid. Some exorcists experience what appears to be the presence of Judas in some cases of possession, but since Judas is human and not demonic, many exorcists believe this is clearly a case of the demon lying. Other exorcists are confused by what seem to be clear signs that this is indeed Judas who is acting. Regardless, there appears to be a good solution for the exorcist when this entity makes an appearance: ask the help of St. Matthias, the apostle who replaced Judas among the Twelve. See Charles D. Fraune, *Slaying Dragons: What Exorcists See and What We Should Know* (Charlotte, NC: Slaying Dragons Press, 2019), 64–65, for a discussion on whether the souls of the damned can possess people.

[99] Fr. Chad Ripperger, "Fr. Ripperger's Widest Range of Topics in One Show."

was that she feared, "Treason."[100] By her victorious death as a martyr in this situation, she conquered this fear and this demon. As Father concluded, "So that's why she became that nemesis."[101]

In the end, however, all saints have a role in rescuing us from the grip of our infernal enemy, whether they are specific nemeses or not. As Fr. Athanasius said:

> It seems clear that some of these saints have *merited* the role of assisting in exorcisms due to a specific spiritual victory over the devil. However, some have merited this involvement as a result of their radical poverty of spirit, their love for Our Lord, or their profound spiritual life. By this, they were a source of vexation for the demons while on earth and they remain that way from Heaven.[102]

Moreover, Fr. Pius cautioned, "While I think the idea that saints are established as the nemeses of certain demons is, in fact, a reality, I think it is something that is not meant for us to dwell on, to understand, or even to know about."[103] Instead, he suggested that faithful Catholics should "invoke the saints that they're fond of and who are already involved in their lives."[104] After all, it is the very nature of the saint—his or her humility, selflessness, and

---

[100] Fr. Chad Ripperger, "Our Lady of Sorrows and Healing."

[101] Fr. Chad Ripperger, "Fr. Ripperger's Widest Range of Topics in One Show."

[102] Fr. Athanasius, in discussion with Charles D. Fraune, July 2024.

[103] Fr. Pius, in discussion with Patrick O'Hearn, September 2024.

[104] Ibid. We also wish to emphasize that in the realm of spiritual warfare, it's important to avoid an unhealthy curiosity that seeks to understand everything about the workings of demons. As Fr. Pius mentioned, some things will always remain a mystery. Instead, the faithful should focus on growing in holiness, which includes forming a strong devotion to the saints.

love of God — that gives him or her power over the forces of evil, and so each is a nemesis of the devil.

The Power of Relics

As an extension of this nemesis relationship, the bodies of the saints (first-class relics) are also utilized in exorcisms in order to apply the merits the saints won in this life against the power of the demon. The saints are invisible; their souls now enjoy the Beatific Vision as they live as glorified members of the Mystical Body of Christ; but they still have a connection to the bodies they possessed in their earthly lives. The body of a person is not a long-forgotten shell that had merely imprisoned the soul in this life, as various heresies believe. Instead, it is an integral part of the person himself: man's nature is a union of body and soul.[105]

The Church has therefore believed since her beginning that the bodies of the saints are sacred and worthy of veneration because these bodies share, in a mysterious way, in the effects of the holiness of the soul, which is now united to Almighty God. It was while they lived in these bodies that the saints prayed, did good deeds, performed mighty miracles, and merited their high place in Heaven. Thus, their bodies participate in their merit. The teaching that the bodies of the saints are to be venerated and honored was solemnly upheld by the Holy Church at the Ecumenical Council of Trent in 1563, which stated:

> The holy bodies of holy martyrs, and of others now living with Christ — which bodies were the living members

---

[105] See *Catechism of the Catholic Church* 365: "Spirit and matter, in man, are not two natures united, but rather their union forms a single nature."

of Christ, and the temple of the Holy Ghost, and which are by Him to be raised unto eternal life, and to be glorified—are to be venerated by the faithful; through which (bodies) many benefits are bestowed by God on men.[106]

Among these benefits are healings, many and various miracles, and aid to exorcists in driving out demons.

As a result, it has been an established practice, mentioned in the instructions for the Rite of Exorcism, that if relics are available, the exorcist should apply these sacred objects to the body of the possessed in a reverent way during the ritual.[107] This practice, as with the use of the Litany of the Saints, has ancient origins. As the Church grew, it was clear that miracles abounded not only through the prayers of holy men and women but also at the tombs of these same revered Christians. The tombs and the remains of the saints (relics) became a source for countless miracles, including physical healings and the exorcism of demons from the possessed, and so the relics of saints were recognized as having great spiritual power over the devil.[108]

We've seen how exorcists try to discover if any one saint in particular seems to irritate a demon, and if this is the case, the exorcist will not only repeatedly invoke that saint but will, if possible, also seek to acquire that saint's relic. In a sense, it is like a

---

[106] Council of Trent, Session 25, "On the Invocation, Veneration, and Relics of Saints, and on Sacred Images."

[107] "If relics of the saints are available, they are to be applied in a reverent way to the chest or the head of the person possessed (the relics must be properly and securely encased and covered). One will see to it that these sacred objects are not treated improperly or that no injury is done them by the evil spirit" (*The Roman Ritual*, vol. 2, 171n13).

[108] Blai, *The History of Exorcism*, 64.

doctor attempting to figure out what is wrong with a patient. The exorcist and his team are trying to discern which demonic "virus" is at work and determine the quickest and most effective saintly "remedy" that will help liberate that soul. Adam Blai said, "If a particular demon is present and we know what that demon does, we get a relic of a saint that overcame that vice or temptation in life. Like, if it's a demon that inspires drinking or drug use you might get St. John Vianney."[109] Fr. Alphonsus explained, "The exorcist will touch the relics to a possessed person and there is often more of a reaction from certain relics than from others.... When there is a reaction, this is another way of knowing that, yes, this is a saint that we really need to appeal to."[110] This reaction to relics also highlights what motivates the demons and shows us how they really are seeking to destroy mankind and prevent us from attaining the glory that Christ has offered us.

Relics are powerful because they are "our real tangible connections with real living saints in Heaven from when they were on earth," Fr. Pius added. "And the demons just hate all of that; they hate everything material because it's just so disgusting to them. It reminds them of the fact that human nature was glorified above their own nature through the Immaculate Conception and through the Incarnation; that's what they hate, because it's humiliating to them." Relics are therefore hated by the enemy and a powerful tool in exorcisms because they humiliate the demons to the point of torture, which then "speeds their departure."[111]

All exorcists report witnessing a powerful response from demons when a relic is brought forth. Fr. Szada, for example,

---

[109] Adam Blai, in discussion with Patrick O'Hearn, October 2024.
[110] Fr. Alphonsus, in discussion with Charles D. Fraune, August 2024.
[111] Fr. Pius, in discussion with Patrick O'Hearn, September 2024.

provided a powerful testimony of the mysterious power that relics wield against the demonic.

Just to show you how powerful relics are, I was interviewing an individual who ultimately did turn out to be possessed. We were in the Church, and I had my team members with me. I'm in the pew, she was in the pew, and behind me, and behind the possessed, two of my team members were in a pew. One of these team members (two women) had a bag with a first-class relic in it. During the course of my interview with the possessed, the team member gently leaned forward and placed this bag against the back of the pew that this person was sitting in. The person screamed, jumped up, flew out into the aisle, and said, "What was that? What did you do? What did you hit me with?" She didn't know it was there and yet she reacted and responded to it: "It stung. It hurt." That was a pretty good indication that she was possessed. She had that knowledge of something and that reaction to the sacred. So that's where we sometimes use those kinds of things as a way of ascertaining whether it really is an authentic case of possession or not. To see those kinds of things can be helpful, even in terms of diagnostics.[112]

Likewise, Fr. Pius explained, "When I bring relics into the exorcisms, the demoniacs writhe beneath the reliquary. They feel like it's burning their skin, despite the fact that it is sitting

---

[112] Fr. John Szada, in discussion with Patrick O'Hearn, August 2024. Remember that, particularly in the United States, there must always be a psychological evaluation of the potentially possessed person before an exorcism is permitted to take place.

on the altar or nearby. They scorn it, spit at it, and generally disdain it."[113]

The specific relics exorcists use depends on which ones they have access to. Some exorcists network with other priests and are able to share relics. Many exorcists have a relic of the True Cross. Fr. Szada has a relic of St. John the Baptist and St. Mary of Jesus Crucified.[114] Fr. Pius has, among many others, relics of Pope St. John Paul II, St. Padre Pio, St. Gemma Galgani, and St. Norbert.[115] Fr. Lampert said he also makes use of a relic of St. Thérèse of Lisieux.[116] Fr. Pius said that a demoniac reacted to St. Robert Bellarmine in the Litany of the Saints, so he made sure he brought that relic to the next session.[117]

Yet the relic that most exorcists keep with them is not from a saint but rather from a stone from the Sanctuary of Monte Sant'Angelo in Gargano, Italy.

Stones from St. Michael's Cave

"Exorcists all over the world have used stones from the cave at Gargano," Blai explained. "The stones are not an instant exorcism for the possessed, but they do act in a similar way to first-class relics of saints that are commonly used in exorcisms."[118] Fr. Ripperger

---

[113] Fr. Pius, in discussion with Patrick O'Hearn, September 2024.

[114] Fr. John Szada, in discussion with Patrick O'Hearn, August 2024.

[115] Fr. Pius, in discussion with Patrick O'Hearn, September 2024.

[116] Fr. Vincent Lampert, in discussion with Patrick O'Hearn, August 2024.

[117] Fr. Pius, in discussion with Patrick O'Hearn, September 2024.

[118] Adam Blai, *The Catholic Guide to Miracles: Separating the Authentic from the Counterfeit* (Manchester, NH: Sophia Institute Press, 2021), 63.

explained that these stones are so powerful because they act as "quasi-relics of St. Michael."[119] He added, "Those stones have a tremendous impact in our line of work."[120] Fr. Lampert agreed, stating, "I use that stone from Monte Sant'Angelo; it seems to be very powerful."[121]

St. Michael first appeared near this cave on Mt. Gargano, in southern Italy, to Bishop Maiorano of Sipontum in 490, at which time the bishop dedicated a church in honor of the archangel at the site of the apparition. St. Michael then appeared again over a thousand years later to Bishop Puccinelli in 1656, when he promised that stones taken from the cave would assist in deliverance prayers and exorcisms.[122]

Fr. Ripperger told a fascinating story about the first time he made use of this stone in an exorcism:

> The first time I really noticed its impact was when I had a woman who was, in my own estimation, [dealing with] a very low-level form of possession.... I prayed over her three times. The third time we prayed, I had actually just gotten the stone [for the first time], I said, "Well, here, hold this," and I started the exorcism of the Apostate Angels, by Pope Leo XIII,[123] which actually starts out with a prayer to St. Michael. I got a third of the way through that prayer

---

[119] Fr. Chad Ripperger, "Exclusive Interview with Renowned Exorcist Fr. Chad Ripperger," interview by Adrian Milag, April 18, 2024, by Adrian Milag TV, YouTube, https://www.youtube.com/watch?v=jZYLWU4pvcs.

[120] Ibid.

[121] Fr. Vincent Lampert, in discussion with Patrick O'Hearn, August 2024.

[122] Adam Blai, *The Catholic Guide to Miracles*, 63.

[123] The prayer in the ritual just after the Rite of Exorcism.

to St. Michael and, as she was holding the stone, both of us experienced this popping sensation, and we both kind of jerked at the same time. We finished the prayers, and from that point on, she was liberated. So it does have a tremendous impact. You see [that] the demons can't stand it in [our] sessions; it just drives them nuts. So it's a very powerful relic.[124]

His report of the "popping sensation" is reminiscent of the account provided by the exorcists who were involved in the exorcism of "Robby," the true story that formed the basis for the movie *The Exorcist*. The end of Robby's possession also involved the intervention of St. Michael, who commanded the demon to finally leave, and at the demon's departure, a sound like a gunshot was heard in the hospital and at the nearby church where other priests were praying.

And so the faithful can take great comfort in St. Michael's power over evil, and we can rejoice that Divine Providence has seen fit to allow this glorious archangel to provide us with the magnificent gift of these stones, whose efficacy is witnessed by priests all over the world.[125]

Stories of Relics in Exorcisms

Because exorcists frequently utilize relics in their work of expelling demons, they have witnessed many fascinating demonstrations of their power.

---

[124] Fr. Chad Ripperger, "Exclusive Interview with Renowned Exorcist Fr. Chad Ripperger."

[125] See Appendix D for instructions on how to purchase a stone from the cave of St. Michael.

Relics of the Blessed Virgin Mary or of St. Joseph, for example, have proven to be highly efficacious in exorcisms. Fr. Pius uses a relic of St. Joseph's staff, which he says "is particularly hated by certain demons."[126] He is also in possession of a relic of part of the veil that Our Lady wore, which is also hated by certain demons. He said, "That relic of the veil of the Blessed Virgin Mary was one that they really despised. They said it made them feel like they were burning. They couldn't stand to be in the presence of it or to be touched by it."[127]

Another saint whose relics seem to hold great power over evil is Pope St. John Paul II. Fr. Lampert shared a story of a time when a relic of this saintly vicar of Christ helped him in an exorcism:

> I worked with somebody one time, and St. John Paul II was the one who really brought the demons out. You can tell that the demons were there, they were kind of mani-festing, but when the relic of St. John Paul II was placed on the body of the possessed person, that was when the demons just completely went ballistic. Of course, I use that information to know, then, obviously, that St. John Paul II is going to be a powerful ally in casting this particular demon out.[128]

Pope St. John Paul II was famous for his uniquely vibrant papacy and reputation for holiness during his earthly life, so it makes sense that he is now one of the key saints to assist exorcists in their work.

---

[126] Fr. Pius, in discussion with Patrick O'Hearn, September 2024.
[127] Ibid.
[128] Fr. Vincent Lampert, in discussion with Patrick O'Hearn, August 2024.

St. Peter's relics are also extremely effective in exorcisms — this should come as no surprise given that he is one of the few saints to be named in the Rite of Exorcism. Msgr. Rossetti shared this story:

> I laid the theca[129] on the temple of the afflicted person, and the body visibly jerked. I commanded him to tell us which saint it was (keeping the theca's identity hidden), and he said, "Peter." Demons aren't psychic per se, but they know some things that are hidden to humans. Clearly, this relic was causing the demons considerable distress.[130]

Another saint who is often interceding in exorcisms is St. Mary of Jesus Crucified, a Carmelite nun from the Middle East. Adam Blai shared a story of how he used one of her first-class relics both to assist people who were seeking general spiritual healing as well as in the Rite of Exorcism:

> I have shared a first-class relic of St. Mary of Jesus Cruci-fied with a number of people who needed healing. In each case, it helped the person when he slept with the relic on his person overnight. One person experienced a complete healing of a year-long untreatable migraine. Another person's medically unexplained chest pains ceased. A third person experienced a spiritual healing. Finally, while being used during a solemn exorcism (in which I applied it to the possessed person's head without saying what the relic was or showing it to him), the relic caused a demon immediately to rage while stamping the floor and shouting, "That nun! That nun! She is helping

---

[129] One of the terms used to designate a container for a relic. Also known as a reliquary.
[130] Rossetti, *Diary of an American Exorcist*, 255.

the Christians in the Middle East die well! She is making them saints! That nun is stealing so many souls from us! That nun! THAT NUN!"[131]

It is not the case, however, that every relic will be of benefit to every exorcist. Fr. Timothy shared a rather comical incident from when he was a new exorcist that demonstrates this reality.

In one exorcism, when I was very new, I was using a relic of St. Elizabeth Ann Seton, thinking, "Oh, this ought to really work." I touched the relic to the back of the energumen's head but there was no reaction, nothing. Confused, and *new*, I tapped on the relic and blew on it, as if to clear it of any dust (as if the dust was the problem!), and tried again. Still, nothing, and I was even more confused. Anyway, I put that relic down and took a simple relic of St. Teresa of Calcutta, a single strand of hair from her head, and placed that relic to the back of the energumen's head. The reaction from the demon was intense, screaming like crazy, saying, "Get that little one, get away from me!"[132]

Still, we can rest assured that there is extraordinary power in using relics in exorcisms, and this effect is not limited only to the bodics of saints. Indeed, while most relics are of the first-class, meaning that they are part of the saint's body, third-class relics have also proven to be powerful, as seen in this story by Fr. Lampert about St. Padre Pio:

I have a scapular that was given to me when I was visiting San Giovanni Rotondo. The priest took the scapular, and

---

[131] Blai, *The Catholic Guide to Miracles*, 22.
[132] Fr. Timothy, in discussion with Charles D. Fraune, August 2024.

he touched it to one of the gloves that Padre Pio wore, and then he gave that to me. So I've done exorcisms where I've actually placed that scapular in my hand and then on the head of the possessed person, and then the person will shriek.[133]

One of the things that most fascinates Catholics today about the testimonies of exorcists is that their anecdotes present a living witness to the power wielded by the spiritual tools of the Church. Relics are clearly among these tools, and these stories of their power can inspire Catholic Christians to grow in gratitude and reverence toward these gifts and to increase their love and honor for the saints, who are our most powerful friends.

The saints cooperated with the grace of God during their earthly lives and so merited to be raised up to be like Him and to work with Him in eternal glory. As such, they are terrifying to the enemy, and they hold great power against the demons. If we likewise cooperate in God's plan of redemption and unite ourselves to His holiness, He can raise us up and empower us to crush all of the devil's specific traps and attacks against us. Then our victories, along with the victories of all the saints, can be used by God to benefit the Church until the end of time.

[133] Fr. Vincent Lampert, in discussion with Patrick O'Hearn, August 2024.

4

Saints Conquer Satan

The saints conquered Satan while they were alive on earth, and they continue to battle their ancient foe from the celestial heights of Heaven.

Scripture teaches us that the saints had the power to conquer Satan "by the blood of the Lamb and by the word of their testimony, for they loved not their lives even unto death" (Rev. 12:11). They partook of Jesus' Body and Blood at Mass, and they sacrificed their lives for the salvation of souls. Some saints, the "red martyrs," literally poured out their blood for Jesus rather than deny Him, and other saints sacrificed their lives daily as "white martyrs," remaining faithful to Christ until the end without shedding their blood. Above all, however, the saints allowed themselves to be conquered by Christ, who is the ultimate victor over evil. They did not live for this world; they lived for the world without end.

The saints fought Satan and his minions until their last breaths. They took Christ's words literally when He said, "He who loves his life loses it, and he who hates his life in this world will keep it for eternal life" (John 12:25). To win the world for Christ, the saints first conquered their own passions and sins. They knew overcoming vice was far harder than defeating Satan, whom they could repel by invoking the Lord. On the other hand, true victory over sin required a lifetime of prayer, fasting, virtue, and grace.

The saints were also not surprised by the machinations of the devil. They understood that God allows the devil to tempt and even possess a body to help a person become holy, and so the devil acts to his own detriment. As Fr. Amorth explained, quoting St. John Chrysostom, "The devil is a sanctifier of souls despite himself, because he is defeated and causes suffering in these holy people who know how to offer their suffering to the Lord, making of it a means of sanctification."[134]

Yet the saints never boasted about defeating their foe, Satan, because they understood that all their power depended on "the blood of the Lamb," and they took to heart Jesus' words to His apostles: "Behold, I have given you authority to tread upon serpents and scorpions, and over all the power of the enemy; and nothing shall hurt you. Nevertheless do not rejoice in this, that the spirits are subject to you; but rejoice that your names are written in heaven" (Luke 10:19–20). And so Jesus reminds us that true victory is not in power over the enemy but in our eternal destiny. But this victory is not automatic—it requires our cooperation. Just like the saints, we also have a choice: conquer the devil or be conquered.

Saints Who Were Exorcists

To be chosen by God as an official exorcist, one who is tasked with confronting the demonic head-on by means of the Church's Rite of Exorcism, is a call within a call; that is, the priest is directly

---

[134] Fr. Gabrielle Amorth, *Get Behind Me, Satan*, trans. Nicholas Reitzug (Manchester, NH: Sophia Institute Press, 2023), 63.

chosen by one's bishop. For this reason, while many saints have cast out the devil, only a handful of saints were exorcists.

The following saints are some of the many who were also exorcists: St. Anthony of Egypt (251–356 A.D.), St. Peter the Exorcist (d. 304 A.D.), St. Benedict (480–547), Bl. William of Toulouse (1297–1369), St. Norbert (1080–1134), and St. Francis Borgia (1510–1572).[135] In modern times, we also have the incredible example of the Servant of God, Fr. Candido Amantini (1914–1992), the teacher and friend of Fr. Amorth. These holy men courageously confronted the powers of darkness, and each played a unique role in the Church's mission of spiritual warfare.

St. Anthony of Egypt (A.D. 251–356)

After the death of his wealthy Christian parents, St. Anthony, also known as Antony, came to a crossroads: Would he serve God in the world, or take a more radical path?

One day, as St. Anthony was pondering how the apostles followed the Lord in such a close way, he entered a church and heard the words of Jesus in St. Matthew's Gospel: "If you would be perfect, go, sell what you possess and give to the poor, and you will have treasure in heaven; and come, follow me" (Matt. 19:21). And so this powerful warrior of God decided to take the road less traveled and gave away everything to follow Him who is perfect.

He first lived among the tombs before retreating to the desert, and he spent nearly twenty years in solitude. During his time in the desert, the devil physically attacked and tempted him in every way.

---

[135] See Philip Kosloski, "5 Saints Who Were Exorcists," *Aleteia* (June 29, 2018), https://aleteia.org/2018/06/29/5-saints-who-were -exorcists.

Yet his holiness drew and inspired other monks, who asked him to be their spiritual father. St. Anthony always gave these monks the same guidance: trust and love God, guard your senses, fast, pray constantly (especially the Psalms), keep the Commandments, shun vainglory, recall the saints' lives, and never go to sleep in anger.[136]

St. Anthony was also an exorcist who brought spiritual healing to those who sought his aid. St. Athanasius described the following account:

> Another time, when he had gone down to the outer monasteries and was asked to enter a ship and pray with the monks, he alone perceived a horrible, pungent smell. The crew said that there was fish and pickled meat in the boat and that the smell was from them, but he said it was different; and even as he spoke, came a sudden shriek from a young man having a devil, who had come on board earlier and was hiding in the vessel. Being charged in the name of our Lord Jesus Christ, the devil went out, and the man was made whole, and all knew that the foul smell was from the evil spirit.[137]

St. Anthony's power was rooted in his trust in God. He never feared the devil, because He knew that the devil was powerless, for Christ had already conquered him.

St. Peter the Exorcist (d. A.D. 304)

Martyred under the Emperor Diocletian, St. Peter the Exorcist remains relatively forgotten compared to many other saints, yet

---

[136] St. Athanasius, *St. Antony of the Desert*, 65.
[137] Ibid., 73.

he, alongside St. Marcellinus, played a pivotal role in the early Church, and he is one of the few saints in the Early Church designated as an exorcist.

Born in Rome in the third century, St. Peter helped liberate many from demonic possession. When he and Marcellinus, a priest, were arrested for being Christians, they saw their imprisonment as an opportunity to spread the Faith, and they converted the jailer and his family. Finally, after Peter and Marcellinus continued to refuse to renounce their faith, they were beheaded in the woods so as to prevent the veneration of their bodies. Two women discovered their bodies, however, and both men were given a proper burial.

So powerful is St. Peter the Exorcist that his name is included in the Roman Canon (Eucharistic Prayer 1) just after St. Marcellinus. St. Peter the Exorcist's unwavering faith and triumph over diabolical forces testify to his power in conquering Satan, and his legacy endures to this day through his veneration in the Church.

St. Benedict (480–547)

St. Benedict, the founder of western monasticism, battled the devil throughout his life, and he possessed a remarkable power to drive out the devil through his own prayers.

The Life of St. Benedict by St. Gregory the Great includes a few stories of demonic attacks. In one case, the devil incited an envious, heretical, Arian priest, Florentius, to offer St. Benedict a poisoned loaf of bread. As if that weren't enough, he then provoked Florentius to send seven naked women into the cloister garden to try to tempt St. Benedict and his monks. The devil also stirred a group of monks to give St. Benedict poisoned wine, but after he made the sign of the cross, the glass shattered. St. Benedict also drove the devil out of people. St. Gregory the Great related the following story:

> One day as he was going to St. John's Oratory, which stands upon the very top of the mountain, he met the old enemy upon a mule in the habit and guise of a physician, carrying a horn and a mortar; who, being demanded whither he went, answered he was going to the monks to minister a drink. Thereupon the venerable Father Benedict went forward to the chapel to pray and, having finished, returned back in great haste, for the wicked spirit found one of the senior monks drawing water, and presently he entered into him, threw him on the ground and tortured him unmercifully. As soon as the man of God, returning from prayer, found him thus cruelly tortured, he only gave him a blow on the cheek with his hand and immediately drove the wicked spirit out of him, so that he never dared to return again.[138]

Today, St. Benedict is the patron saint of exorcists, and his fight against the devil wages on from Heaven.

Bl. William of Toulouse (1297–1369)

Bl. William joined the Augustinian Order around the age of nineteen. He studied in Paris but lived mostly in Toulouse, France, in the monastery of Saint'Etienne. Although little is known about his life, Bl. William was a gifted preacher and spiritual director, devoted to prayer and penance, and his sermons inspired many to enter religious life. He loved reading the lives of the saints

---

[138] St. Gregory the Great, *The Life of St. Benedict*, 41.

as he sought to follow their path of virtue. He also had a deep devotion to Mary under the title of "Sorrowful Mother" and to the Holy Souls in Purgatory.

During his life, Bl. William helped deliver people from demonic possession, and he himself was often beset by demons who visibly appeared to him and tried to harm him. With God's help, and strengthened by a life of mortification and simplicity, he resisted every temptation. Bl. William passed away in Toulouse on May 18, 1369, and he was buried in his monastic cemetery. After many miracles occurred through his intercession, his body was moved to the chapel of St. Mary Magdalene, where he had frequently celebrated Mass. Pope Leo XIII later declared him Blessed in 1893. Victorious over the devil and the power of sin, Bl. William now intercedes for exorcists and those facing possession and temptation.

St. Norbert (ca. 1080–1134)

St. Norbert was born in the Rhineland (western Germany) into a noble family, and he spent his youth seeking the pleasures of life. One day, however, St. Norbert was thrown off his horse during a thunderstorm. After lying unconscious on the ground for an hour, he awoke and cried out, "Lord, what wouldst thou have me to do?" To which St. Norbert heard interiorly, "Turn away from evil, and do good: seek after peace, and pursue it."[139]

After St. Norbert recovered from his brush with death, he devoted himself to prayer and penance and spent long periods

[139] "St. Norbert," *EWTN*, https://www.ewtn.com/catholicism/saints /norbert-712.

of retreat at the abbey of Siegburg near Cologne. Eventually, he became a priest.

St. Norbert then traveled throughout Europe preaching the gospel until the bishop of Laon, France, offered him land to start his own religious community in the Prémontré valley. St. Norbert began his order with thirteen canons. The order wore distinctive white habits in imitation of the holy angels, and they grew quickly. St. Norbert was also instrumental in helping heal a schism that occurred after the death of Pope Honorius II.

St. Norbert was one of the premiere exorcists of his day, and his official medieval biography, the *Vita Norberti*, is a rich source of information about exorcism in the twelfth century. One particular exorcism involved a twelve-year-old, possessed girl who was liberated at Nivelles (in present-day Belgium). The possessed girl's father brought her to St. Norbert after she had been tormented by a demon for over a year, during which time the girl had to be locked in chains. St. Norbert began by reading the Gospel. The devil then mocked St. Norbert by reciting the entire Canticle of Canticles in French and German. The possessed girl then tried to choke St. Norbert with his stole. Those present attempted to free St. Norbert, but he declared, "Don't! Let her be! If she has received the power from God, let her do what she can."[140] At those words, the devil ceased his attack on St. Norbert. The exorcism continued. St. Norbert had the girl placed in holy water and had her blonde hair cut so that the devil could not use it to control her. Night approached, and St. Norbert was upset that the demon had not left. He told the father to bring his daughter

---

[140] *The Life of Saint Norbert, Founder of the Order of Prémontré*, trans. Rev. Theodore J. Antry (Bethlehem Priory of St. Joseph, Tehachapi, CA, 2021), chap. 22, no. 46.

back tomorrow for Mass, and he promised to fast until the girl was healed.

During Mass on the following day, St. Norbert had two of his confreres hold the possessed girl down close to the altar. He continued to read the Gospel over the girl, but it was not until the consecration that the devil's power began to shatter. The demon shouted, "Look, look how he holds his little God in his hands."[141] St. Norbert intensified his prayer. The demon then cried out, "I'm burning, I'm burning." Next, the demon said, "I'm dying, I'm dying." And finally, the demon shouted in a loud voice, "I want to leave, I want to leave, let me go."[142]

St. Norbert's authority over demons was not merely a matter of words but of deep spiritual discipline. He lived a life of intense prayer and fasting, and he fully embraced the Lord's call to self-denial. Like the disciples who once asked Jesus why they could not cast out a demon, St. Norbert understood the answer firsthand: "This kind cannot be driven out by anything but prayer and fasting" (Mark 9:29). His strength as an exorcist came not from his own power but from his profound union with God—one forged through unwavering devotion, mortification, and trust in divine grace.

St. Francis Borgia (1510–1572)

Before being elected as the third Superior General of the Society of Jesus, also known as the Jesuits, St. Francis Borgia was a

---

[141] Ibid., no. 47. On this note, *The Life of St. Norbert* mentioned that "demons confess what heretics deny," referring to the Real Presence of Jesus in the Holy Eucharist.
[142] Ibid.

husband and the father of eight children. After the unexpected passing of his wife, Eleanor, however, St. Francis Borgia withdrew from worldly life and, after ensuring that his children were well provided for, joined religious life at the age of thirty-nine.

St. Francis Borgia was instrumental in sending missionaries throughout the world during the sixteenth century. He was friends with St. Ignatius of Loyola, and he battled the devil and sought to free others from demonic possession:

> Among his many gifts, St. Francis Borgia possessed that of exercising great power over evil spirits. One special instance is recorded, in which several bishops and persons eminent for sanctity having altogether failed, by the use of the exorcisms prescribed by the Church, to deliver an unhappy man from the demon which had tormented him for years, Francis was requested to pray for the afflicted creature. He could not refuse, and at the close of his prayer he laid his hand on the head of the possessed, pronouncing at the same time the words of our Lord: *In nomine meo daemonia ejicient*—"In My Name shall they cast out devils." Forthwith the devil departed, to the astonishment of the bystanders, who could not help giving expression to their admiration for Francis' virtue, which imparted such efficacy to his prayers. "How can you wonder," he replied, "that the devil should fly before me? *Two of a trade never agree!* Alas for me! During many years my business was the same as his, for I too was a tempter of souls, giving a bad example, and leading many to their ruin."[143]

---

[143] A. M. Clarke, *The Life of St. Francis Borgia* (London: Burns and Oates, Limited, 1894), 317–318.

The life of St. Francis Borgia therefore demonstrates that even saints were once enslaved by Satan, since "He who commits sin is of the devil, for the devil has sinned from the beginning" (1 John 3:8). Yet St. Francis Borgia strove never to commit a mortal sin. By standing with Christ and avoiding sin at all costs, he became the devil's foe.

From his youth, St. Francis Borgia was acutely aware of the devil:

> I acknowledge that I received signal graces from God when out in the open country. Many a time, watching the birds at conflict in the air, I bethought me of the work of the devil in destroying souls; what wide circuits he makes in search of them, how swiftly he swoops down on them, how fiercely he attacks them, how he struggles to obtain the mastery, and how vigilant he is to prevent them from escaping from his talons.[144]

These experiences prepared him to become an exorcist, but one story is particularly worth noting. Before his death, St. Francis Borgia entrusted his sister-in-law with his most beloved possession: his crucifix. This miraculous crucifix had once shed drops of blood from Jesus' five sacred wounds while in the presence of an unrepentant sinner. The crucifix later made its way to South America through one of St. Francis's grandsons, where it continued to work miracles:

> We find, however, the case mentioned of a man possessed by the devil, upon whom every form of exorcism sanctioned by the Church had been tried in vain. When the crucifix which had belonged to St. Francis was placed in a

---

[144] Ibid., 34.

room next to that in which he was, he evinced the utmost terror, uttering a series of unearthly shrieks, and writhing on the ground in contortions terrible to behold. Yet he had never seen this crucifix, nor even heard of it, nor was it possible, humanly speaking, that he could have become aware of its proximity. When the paroxysm had subsided, the enemy of souls was forced, through the mouth of his wretched victim, to render unequivocal testimony to the eminent sanctity of the great servant of God.[145]

Servant of God Candido Amantini (1914–1992)

Servant of God Fr. Candido Amantini was the chief exorcist for the Diocese of Rome for thirty-six years. His most famous pupil, Fr. Gabriele Amorth, would go on to become Rome's main exorcist and the founder of the International Association of Exorcists.

Fr. Candido had a special gift of discerning who was possessed. He would simply say a brief prayer and look at a person's face and know whether he or she was afflicted by a demon. According to Fr. Amorth, he could even diagnose a case by looking at a photograph of a person's eyes.[146] Because he was able to determine demonic possession so quickly, he was able to meet with around eighty people each morning, although he excused himself from exorcisms on Sundays. Each night, Fr. Candido would make a holy hour in the chapel to be strengthened for spiritual combat.[147]

---

[145] Ibid., 106.

[146] Fr. Gabriele Amorth and Marcello Stanzione, *The Devil Is Afraid of Me*, 18.

[147] Fr. Gabriele Amorth, with Elisabetta Fezzi, *Father Amorth: My Battle against Satan*, trans. Charlotte J. Fasi (Manchester, NH: Sophia Institute Press, 2018), 39.

Fr. Candido was also friends with St. Padre Pio, who sometimes advised him in his exorcisms. As Fr. Candido once recounted to Fr. Amorth:

I was exorcising him like a Greco-Roman wrestling match, and I did not know who would be checked off. At times, there are people who are truly violent, and if a priest exorcist does not know ahead of time how to protect himself, for example, with personal assistants, he could find himself in a bad way. In this case … at a certain point, this young man collapsed, and I collapsed around him. And whoever might have witnessed it would not have understood who was the exorcist and who was the person being exorcised. Padre Pio sent me a note saying: "Dear Father, it is useless for you to waste time and effort with that young man. There is nothing that can be done!" And I asked him: Why? He said the young man was an impenitent womanizer. He did not try to conquer his vice, and when one lives habitually in a state of sin, the exorcisms do not count for anything.[148]

Fr. Amorth also noted how Fr. Candido "received assaults from the devil on his deathbed,"[149] and even after Fr. Candido's passing in 1992, Fr. Amorth insisted that his help in exorcisms continued:

Padre Pio was present in the same way that Father Candido was present so many other times, and the demon would shout: "Away with that priest, away with that priest!" "Who is he?" I would ask, "Father Candido?" "Yes, yes, it

---

[148] Amorth and Stanzione, *The Devil Is Afraid of Me*, 61–62.
[149] Amorth, *My Battle against Satan*, 40.

is." Well, then, if the two of them are with me when I do the exorcisms, I am well placed![150]

Prayer is what made Fr. Candido fearsome to the demons; and now Fr. Candido's intercession continues. As St. Padre Pio said, and as it now reads on his tombstone, "Father Candido is truly a priest according to the heart of God." His cause for beatification was introduced in 2012.

Patron Saints for the Possessed

Catholics would do well to invoke the above saints in their own spiritual battles, as they were fearsome against Satan. The Church also recognizes additional patron saints against demonic possession, such as St. Amabilis of Auvergne, St. Cyriacus the Martyr, St. Bruno, St. Denis of Paris, St. Dymphna, St. Lucian, St. Lupus of Troyes, St. Marcian, St. Margaret of Fontana, St. Quirinus of Sescia, St. Ubaldus Baldassini, and Bl. Lucy Bufalari. These holy men and women have some association with the demonic: perhaps they drove away demons by their prayers or dabbled with the diabolical before their conversion. For instance, St. Margaret of Fontana and St. Paul of the Cross drove the devil away by the Sign of the Cross,[151] while St. Marcian was a possible devil worshipper before he converted to Christianity.

Since the battle against Satan involves the battle against sin, saints who have a connection to repentance and the Sacrament

---

[150] Ibid., 25.

[151] Fr. Athanasius further explained that St. John of the Cross was so powerful in his life that he "would walk through the town and the possessed would be liberated" (Fr. Athanasius, in discussion with Charles D. Fraune, July 2024).

of Confession can also be helpful companions, especially those saints who died protecting the seal of Confession, such as St. John Nepomucene. Fr. Pius also recommended St. John Vianney or St. John or the great penitential saints, such as St. Mary Magdalene and St. Mary of Egypt, who both have beautiful stories of humility and repentance.[152]

When Fr. Amorth was once asked which particular saints should be invoked by those who suffer from spiritual evils, he responded:

> I advise invoking those saints who have experienced the same disturbances; for example, Blessed Eustace (in the secular life, Lucrezia Bellini), a Benedictine nun from Padua who lived in the fifteenth century. She died at the age of twenty-five after having been possessed by a demon from the age of four. Her religious life, begun at eighteen, was also heavily conditioned by that grave possession, which she tolerated, offering her sufferings to expiate the sins of those who caused her tribulations. Even her own consecrated sisters mistreated her, annoyed by the disturbances her possession caused the communal life of their convent. Only shortly before her death did they understand that they had been living with a saint. Even today many pray before her tomb in the church of St. Peter, imploring the grace of liberation.[153]

We should keep all these saints in mind not only if or after we experience diabolical attacks, but also to guard ourselves from

---

[152] Fr. Pius, in discussion with Patrick O'Hearn, September 2024.
[153] Amorth, *An Exorcist Explains the Demonic*, 126.

evil and temptation in the first place. God has given us these holy aids so that we may always protect our souls.

Why Certain Saints Show Up

So why do certain saints show up in exorcisms, and how does an exorcist know which saint to invoke in the first place?

Saints are powerful in exorcisms because they spent their lifetime slaying diabolical dragons. For instance, Fr. Pius noted that certain contemporary saints, such as Padre Pio and Gemma Galgani, stand out as especially formidable in exorcisms "because they both had a lot of experiences in their own personal lives of wrestling with demons, even tangibly, physically, visibly wrestling with demons."[154] Yet he added that above all, "In my experience, the intercession of the saints really depends, to some degree, on the person who is possessed and the nature of the demons that are possessing him."[155]

Fr. Szada also emphasized that the nature of the person and their demon is particularly important when an exorcist is trying to determine which saints to call upon for aid:

> One of the questions that you're allowed to ask a possessed person is "what is the name of the demon, the one possessing you?" When you get that name … you have an idea of what it was that caused the possession in the first place. Then you know, from that, which counterbalancing saint to invoke in order to be able to combat that particular demon.[156]

---

[154] Fr. Pius, in discussion with Patrick O'Hearn, September 2024.
[155] Ibid.
[156] Fr. John Szada, in discussion with Patrick O'Hearn, August 2024.

Fr. Lampert added:

> The particular saint may be based on what doorway the person opened[157] that brought in the demonic. There may be a particular saint that was dealing with that [situation] as well; you might think of St. Augustine, for example, who led a pretty wild life early on and then committed himself to Christ. So if you're dealing with somebody who may be leading a life of habitual sin, then St. Augustine, who knew that in his own life, becomes the very powerful ally and presence … even in a more profound way.[158]

When asked about why certain saints stand out, Adam Blai clarified, "It's more about that person than it is about the saints. A person may have a close relationship with a saint, or Jesus wants them to learn more about that saint and pursue conversion through that relationship with that saint."[159] Msgr. Rossetti also noted the importance of invoking the possessed person's favorite saints: "At the beginning of a session, I typically ask the afflicted person if he or she has a devotion to a particular saint. If so, we will invoke that saint during the prayers."[160] Blai was further asked if the exorcist can have any influence on which saints appear. He explained that in the end, it is "not the exorcist's preference. None of us have an impact on which saint God sends."[161]

---

[157] The "doorway" is a reference to the specific sin the person committed that opened him or her to an assault by the demonic.

[158] Fr. Vincent Lampert, in discussion with Patrick O'Hearn, August 2024.

[159] Adam Blai, email message to Patrick O'Hearn, October 22, 2024.

[160] Rossetti, *Diary of an American Exorcist*, 199.

[161] Adam Blai, email message to Patrick O'Hearn, October 2024.

On the other hand, Fr. Amorth believed that exorcists often invoke those saints they are devoted to, but he also emphasized the importance of those saints to whom the possessed person has a devotion.[162] The point is, Heaven stands ready to intervene, regardless of how or which saint is invoked.

Fr. Alphonsus offered an additional insight into why certain saints might appear:

Oh yes, there is often a connection between the saint who appears and the struggles of the possessed person: the saint may have struggled with the same vice that the possessed person struggled with or the saint heroically lived out the virtue that the possessed person needs to develop. It is often connected with one of those two things.

However, at other times, it's just like … who knows! It's kind of like how things just show up in our lives. It's like why this saint from another country shows up, or like St. Sharbel, in my own life a lot of times, he kept showing up in various ways in my life. Then, it's like, "Okay, Okay, I get it. I should have a greater devotion to you!" But, addressing the "why" regarding who shows up at which exorcism, especially when there's nothing that I can find that relates so much to me with that saint's life—I often think, "Well, in Heaven, we'll know! The answer will be given then, but not now.[163]

Ultimately, why God sends certain saints in exorcisms remains a mystery. Yet the saints we are most devoted to gladly come to

---

[162] Amorth, *Get Behind Me, Satan*, 61.
[163] Fr. Alphonsus, in discussion with Charles D. Fraune, August 2024.

our aid, especially in the darkest and most disturbing moments such as demonic possession.

Saintly Presence in Exorcisms

We know that the saints are present in exorcisms, but when do they appear during the rite? How do they make themselves known? Where do they appear in the room? And what do they do once they appear?

The process of liberating someone from possession through the Rite of Exorcism typically progresses through six stages, known as the stages of liberation.[164] During each of these stages, the demon's hold on the person is gradually and more notably weakened, and the exorcist obtains a greater understanding of how to end the particular possession. While the presence of various saints is often noticed during the Litany of the Saints at the beginning of the rite, exorcists have also observed that their activity is especially pronounced during the second part of the fifth stage, also known as the sanctoral stage. As Fr. Ripperger once recounted,

> This is when saints will appear; not to me, I don't see them, they appear to the person who's possessed and to the demon. In one of the last cases I had, when St. Joan of Arc was part of it, she actually appeared to the woman. John Paul II actually appeared to the woman. St. Joseph appeared to the woman during this phase, during this timeline. Our Lady will often appear as well.[165]

---

[164] Fraune, *Slaying Dragons*, 81–86.

[165] Fr. Chad Ripperger, "Levels of Spiritual Warfare & Our Lady," January 25, 2024, by St. Patrick's Cathedral NYC, YouTube, https://www.youtube.com/watch?v=KQOSzZprIO4&t=2972s.

That said, how does an exorcist know if saints are present, especially if they do not see them? Fr. Athanasius explained:

> The exorcist determines that a saint is present by gauging the reactions of the demon and the energumen. Sometimes the demons are forced to say what is happening, but they don't like to. Sometimes the demon, through the energumen, will look over the exorcist's shoulder and scream because they have noticed that a saint is now in the room.[166]

The demons can also reveal their intentions or be commanded by the exorcist to disclose which saint is present. Fr. Timothy related the following story:

> The demons, just before they leave, they scream like crazy and say, "He or she says I have to leave now!" They'll scream it, especially. They're screaming in different ways like, "JPII, we hate you! JPII, we hate you! He says I have to leave!" The demon will say something very clearly and directly, like, "The little one, I hate her so much! The little one, with her blue stripes, I hate her. She says I have to leave!" I will respond, "Oh, do you mean Teresa of Calcutta?" They respond, "Aaah!"
>
> Of course, I don't trust them when they speak, not until the last minute, or when they name something very accurate. As we know, all they want to do is lie and distract, so I don't trust anything they say until about the last five minutes or so before they leave.[167]

---

[166] Fr. Athanasius, in discussion with Charles D. Fraune, July 2024.
[167] Fr. Timothy, in discussion with Charles D. Fraune, August 2024.

Once these saints appear, where are they in the context of the room? Fr. Pius explains that "The demons will see [the saints] over the altar or in the chapel or in part of the room, like in the corner or something like that."[168] His words also emphasize that the best place to perform an exorcism is in a church, chapel, "or other such places specially dedicated to God," as *The Scourge of Demons* states, as these places provide an atmosphere steeped in the sacred and less inclined to scandal or unhelpful distractions.[169]

Finally, what exactly do the saints do when they appear? Some saints manifest powerful signs, as will be examined in the next chapter. But in general, as Fr. Lampert described,

> They just show up—they don't really need to say anything. With the saints, angels, or even fallen angels, they don't communicate verbally. It's almost like just having that intuition, just knowing. That's why I would describe it as "showing up." … They're bringing the glory of God with them. That's what is radiating from them: they're taking that light, if you will, and casting it upon the darkness of the demons.[170]

So while the exorcists do not see or hear the saints, they do feel the saints' presence through the divine glory that they bring. And they feel the saints' presence strongly and frequently throughout the exorcism, especially Our Lady's presence. When asked how regularly he experiences the saints' presence, Fr. Szada declared:

---

[168] Fr. Pius, in discussion with Patrick O'Hearn, September 2024.

[169] Menghi, *The Scourge of Demons*, 71.

[170] Fr. Vincent Lampert, in discussion with Patrick O'Hearn, August 2024.

It's always, because when you're talking about the Communion of Saints, they're always going to be present when these kinds of rituals are involved. As a result, we call upon their power and their intercessory power whenever we have one of these especially difficult sessions. Sometimes the sessions aren't so difficult; sometimes you're dealing with demons who are cowards. The saints are always there, and you always rely upon their intercession to be there with us.[171]

There is a mistaken belief championed by many Protestants that those in Heaven do not concern themselves with this valley of tears. Yet would not a good teammate who crosses the finish line in a cross-country race seek to cheer on those who are still running? Would they not desire their brothers and sisters to be with them? Certainly, they would. The saints who were victorious in their fight against the devil while on earth continue to wield their swords from Heaven, where they not only intercede for us but also show up in exorcisms as advocates for the exorcist and the possessed person.

After all, the saints are the assassins of Satan, and their prayers mow down all diabolical threats.

---

[171] Fr. John Szada, in discussion with Patrick O'Hearn, August 2024.

5

Timeless Saints, Come to Our Aid

In the battle for souls, the Catholic Church elevates the saints as our heavenly friends, intercessors, and warriors in the fight against evil. The Litany of the Saints calls to mind over forty of these saints, nearly all of whom lived many centuries ago. These are the timeless saints—those who lived in ancient or medieval times but who are still actively interceding for us in Heaven and helping us battle the devil on earth.

The saintly names listed in the litany are our ancestors in the Faith. These brave men and women—some apostles, some bishops, some virgins, some martyrs, some monks, some nuns, some laymen—provide a snapshot of the universal Church. Reading the Litany of the Saints is similar to reading the genealogy of Jesus in the opening pages of St. Matthew's Gospel: it shows us God's providential love throughout history through His elected sons and daughters. And these saintly names are powerful.

While the following exorcism stories are by no means exhaustive in naming all the saints who can come to our aid in exorcisms, they will demonstrate to us that these timeless saints have much to teach us in the way of virtue and deliverance. These are not just heroes of old but heroes for all time. The timeless saints are mighty indeed, and the demons hate them.

St. Joseph

In the Litany of the Saints, St. Joseph's name rightly appears near the top, following only Our Lady, the archangels, and St. John the Baptist, since as the foster-father of Jesus, he is considered to be the greatest saint after Our Lady.

St. Joseph has his own litany as well in which he is referred to as the "terror of demons" and the "protector of the Holy Church." As the "terror of demons," St. Joseph stands on the offense, fighting against evil with a mighty power from God. Yet as the "protector of the Holy Church," he also acts defensively, guarding the adopted brothers and sisters of Christ and the sons and daughters of Mary just as he guarded the Holy Family.

St. Joseph feared the Lord and listened to His commands. He fled in the middle of the night to Egypt at the command of an angel to protect his wife and Son from King Herod's attack. He led the Holy Family over one thousand miles from Bethlehem to Egypt and eventually back to Nazareth, defending Mary and the Baby Jesus all the while from potential robbers and dangerous animals. Indeed, long before St. Joseph was born, he was foreshadowed in Psalm 112:1–3:

> Blessed is the man who fears the LORD,
>> who greatly delights in his commandments!
> His descendants will be mighty in the land;
>> the generation of the upright will be blessed.
> Wealth and riches are in his house;
>> and his righteousness endures forever.

Fearing the Lord here means awe and respect for God's majesty. It is one of the seven gifts of the Holy Spirit. Because St. Joseph feared the Lord, the demons feared him, and Scripture promises that we, his spiritual descendants, will be mighty like him if we invoke him and imitate his holiness.

In 1870, Pope Pius IX declared St. Joseph the "Patron of the Universal Church" because St. Joseph protects His Son's Church and every soul within if we but invoke his powerful name. St. Padre Pio spoke of St. Joseph's formidable role in the spiritual combat:

St. Joseph, with the love and generosity with which he guarded Jesus, so too will he guard your soul, and as he defended him from Herod, so will he defend your soul from the fiercest Herod: the devil! All the care that the Patriarch St. Joseph has for Jesus, he has for you and will always help you with his patronage.[172]

Other saints have also testified to how much St. Joseph can help us advance in virtue, and the more we grow in virtue, the less power the devil has over us. As St. Teresa of Ávila once declared,

Would that I could persuade all men to be devout to this glorious saint; for I know by long experience what blessings he can obtain for us from God. I have never known anyone who was really devout to him, and who honored him by particular services, who did not visibly grow more and more in virtue; for he helps in a special way those souls who commend themselves to him. It is now some years since I have always on his feast asked him for something, and I always have it. If the petition be in any way amiss, he directs it aright for my greater good.[173]

Though St. Joseph does not show up frequently in exorcisms, he has revealed himself to many exorcists. "There are many saints

---

[172] Jose A. Rodrigues, *The Book of Joseph: God's Chosen Father* (Toronto, Ontario: Ave Maria Centre of Peace, 2017), 126.

[173] St. Teresa of Ávila, *The Life of St. Teresa of Jesus*, trans. David Lewis (New York: Benziger Brothers, 1910), 38.

that all exorcists are seeing: Pope John Paul II, Padre Pio, and St. Joseph," declared Fr. Athanasius.[174] Fr. Ripperger shared one of the most incredible exorcisms involving St. Joseph:

> Most of the exorcists I talked to say that St. Joseph doesn't really show up a whole lot. But when he does, there's stuff that happens. So in one particular case I had, when he showed up, I didn't know that he had shown up; I did invoke him at certain points during the earlier part of the ritual, but when he showed up during it (of course, I don't see this, it's the possessed person who's seeing what the demon sees), every so often the [possessed] woman would literally just convulse during [the exorcism] … and afterwards, I asked her what happened, and she said, "Well, he appeared, and he had his staff, and every time he would hit the ground," she said, "from the top of my head to the bottom of my feet, just absolute terror would just permeate my whole body."
>
> Of course he's the terror of demons, and then in doing a little bit of research on the staff, it's not just the staff of the correction and guidance, it's actually the staff of punishment too. So that's why they would have so much fear of him. So he is an extraordinarily powerful individual in relationship to this. They fear him tremendously.[175]

Msgr. Rossetti also recounted invoking St. Joseph's intercession due to one afflicted person's particular devotion to him:

> During the session, while the demons were fully manifesting, I invoked St. Joseph. The demons frantically yelled,

---

[174] Fr. Athanasius, in discussion with Charles D. Fraune, July 2024.
[175] Fr. Chad Ripperger, "Fr. Ripperger's Wildest Range of Topics in One Show."

"No. Not him. Stop!" Pressing the advantage, our team prayed again and again and again, "St. Joseph, pray for us. St. Joseph cast out the demons." This afflicted person has made considerable progress in recent days and her life is almost back to normal, with few demonic symptoms.[176]

St. Joseph's other titles in the Litany of the Saints echo his powerful role in the home: foster-father of the Son of God, head of the Holy Family, glory of domestic life, and pillar of families. St. Joseph drives out all the demons that affect our home life and fills our domestic churches with the heavenly presence of Nazareth — one marked by peace, love, and joy. Fr. Szada told one story of St. Joesph showing up in an exorcism that was related to domestic strife:

> The one I'm thinking specifically about was an individual for whom, after our last session, we came to realize, part of the issue was a father-son relationship. Without going into details, we knew that this relationship was at the root of the cause of the possession. So St. Joseph comes in on that one; he has a part to play in establishing a more healthy, balanced relationship.[177]

St. Joseph, the silent warrior of Scripture, is far from quiet today. As the Patron of the Universal Church and Pillar of Families, his powerful role makes him a formidable adversary to the devil and his minions. Those who invoke his intercession are never left unaided. As Fr. Lampert said, "Archbishop Daniel Buechlein ... always used to say about St. Joseph: 'He's slow but sure'; that if you're going to invoke the intercession of St. Joseph, you're in for

---

[176] Rossetti, *Diary of an American Exorcist*, 199.
[177] Fr. John Szada, in discussion with Patrick O'Hearn, August 2024.

the long haul. When you really get him to respond, then watch out. There's that notion of terror of demons once again."[178]

St. Michael the Archangel

St. Michael is not a "saint" in the strictest sense. He has not been canonized because the Catholic Church does not canonize angels. However, the word saint derives from the Latin *sanctus*, meaning "holy, consecrated," and St. Michael the Archangel's holiness has long been recognized by the Catholic Church.

Along with St. Raphael and St. Gabriel, St. Michael, whose name means "who is like God," is one of three archangels mentioned by name in Scripture. In the Book of Revelations, he initiates the charge to drive out the fallen angels from Heaven (12:7–9). He has four main roles or offices in the Catholic Church: Leader of the Army of God, Angel of Death, Weigher of Souls, and Guardian of the Church.[179] As the Leader of God's Army, St. Michael commands the angels in their battle against the demons. As the Angel of Death, he escorts the faithful to Heaven and aids them at the moment of death. As the Weigher of Souls, he plays a role in God's judgment of humanity. Additionally, as the Guardian of the Church, he protects the Body of Christ and defends various cities and nations.[180] So powerful is the name of St. Michael the Archangel that he is listed directly after Our Lady in the Litany of the Saints, even before St. Joseph!

---

[178] Fr. Vincent Lampert, in discussion with Patrick O'Hearn, August 2024.

[179] "St. Michael the Archangel," *Catholic Online*, https://www.catholic .org/saints/saint.php?saint_id=308.

[180] Ibid.

According to Cardinal Nasalli of Bologna, sometime between January 1884 and November 1886, Pope Leo XIII had a vision involving demons congregating (*addensavano*) upon the Eternal City (i.e., Rome). After this vision, Pope Leo composed the famous Prayer to St. Michael; the cardinal further stated that the pope's vision was the inspiration for at least one of the lines in the prayer to St. Michael.[181] Pope Leo XIII also composed a longer exorcism prayer to St. Michael that was added to the *Roman Ritual*. A portion of this prayer reads:

> St. Michael the Archangel,
> illustrious leader of the heavenly army,
> defend us in the battle against principalities and powers,
> against the rulers of the world of darkness
> and the spirit of wickedness in high places.
>
> Come to the rescue of mankind,
> whom God has made in His own image and likeness,
> and purchased from Satan's tyranny at so great a price.
>
> Holy Church venerates you as her patron and guardian.
> The Lord has entrusted to you the task
> of leading the souls of the redeemed to heavenly
> blessedness.
>
> Entreat the Lord of peace to cast Satan down under
>   our feet,
> so as to keep him from further holding man captive and
> doing harm to the Church.

[181] Kevin J. Symonds, *Pope Leo XIII and the Prayer to St. Michael* (Boonville, NY: Preserving Christian Publications, 2018), 1–4, 27–34.

Carry our prayers up to God's throne,
that the mercy of the Lord may quickly come
and lay hold of the beast, the serpent of old, Satan
    and his demons,
casting him in chains into the abyss, so that he can
    no longer seduce the nations.[182]

St. Michael the Archangel was a dragon slayer since before man was created, so it should come as no surprise that he plays a powerful role in exorcisms. Adam Blai testifies:

Even the St. Michael Prayer that the laity can say has had great effect during exorcisms I have attended. Sometimes it is said in the background by the lay assistants while the exorcism is going on. We also regularly use a blessed icon of St. Michael. The theology of blessed icons is that they are a window into the spiritual reality that they depict. We have seen the demons talk to St. Michael in the icon many times, even when the icon is held behind the persons where they cannot see it. The demons have also confessed many times that they fear St. Michael and that he is the greatest of the angels. In one case, a demon was very worn down during the exorcism and very much wanted to leave, and it yelled, "St. Michael, please cast me out!"[183]

Fr. Szada described another instance involving St. Michael and his relic from the cave of St. Michael, which was previously described in chapter 3; yet he clarified that while the relic has extraordinary power, it is not a magical means of instant exorcism:

[182] "Exorcism against Satan and the Fallen Angels," in *The Roman Ritual*, vol. 2, 223.
[183] Blai, *The Catholic Guide to Miracles*, 63-64.

One of my great patrons is St. Michael the Archangel. Of course, he's always very powerful in these sorts of things, but I had one very, very interesting experience. I had been to Italy and to the Cave of St. Michael, down into the caverns where we're allowed to go. I picked up a small stone from the ground, so I knew it wasn't one we got from the gift shop, it was something that I actually got from the ground itself. I had it in a small, plastic case with a clear cover on it, and during one of the exorcisms, I took this case and I placed the case against the forehead of the person who was possessed. When I removed the case, the people in my team gasped because what had happened was the image of the stone, not the case, but the stone, embedded itself in the forehead of the person who was possessed, which was rather fascinating since it was in a case. Unfortunately, that person is still being possessed; it's a very strong case, a very powerful case, that we're having difficulty.[184]

Fr. Benedict likewise noted that he uses the relics in exorcisms, and he said that when he touches the little rocks to a possessed person, the demons go ballistic. He has also seen people healed through the stones, and he has noticed that the stones subdue a possessed person. Finally, Fr. Benedict believed that "it is really good for people to have [the stones] in each of their homes."[185]

Fr. Benedict also emphasized the strength of the Chaplet of St. Michael the Archangel in exorcisms.[186] He contended that

---

[184] Fr. John Szada, in discussion with Patrick O'Hearn, August 2024.

[185] Fr. Benedict, in discussion with Patrick O'Hearn, December 2024.

[186] See appendix E for instructions on how to pray the Chaplet of St. Michael.

"the Chaplet is the most powerful chaplet in the universe next to the Rosary itself. I've had many people set free while praying it or instructing them to pray it. And whatever was obsessing them or hurting them was gone."[187] He told a story about an exorcism in Central America[188] involving two teenagers, one girl and one boy, who had become fully possessed after playing with a Ouija board. Each teenager had to be held down by five grown men. "They were like monsters,"[189] said Fr. Benedict. The bishop asked Fr. Benedict to help since he was the only priest trained in exorcism in his diocese. Fr. Benedict immediately ordered twenty-five prayer warriors to pray the Rosary. He then planted between fifty and one hundred St. Benedict medals, which he called his "spiritual hand grenades,"[190] around the chapel where he would perform the exorcism in order to sanctify and protect the property and cut off all diabolical communication from the children to the surrounding areas.

Upon entering the chapel, the two teenagers in the front pew "reacted like a volcano,"[191] despite neither seeing nor hearing Fr. Benedict approach. The presence of an ordained, faithful Catholic priest clearly had a huge impact on the demons. Fr. Benedict gave

---

[187] Fr. Benedict, in discussion with Patrick O'Hearn, December 2024.

[188] Fr. Benedict worked under total obedience to the local bishop wherever he happened to be traveling and ministering throughout the world. In his own home diocese in Central America, his Ordinary there reviewed every exorcism, endorsing and strongly encouraging his ministry; indeed, every case of demonization in that diocese was referred to Fr. Benedict's office.

[189] Fr. Benedict, in discussion with Patrick O'Hearn, December 2024.

[190] Ibid.

[191] Ibid.

them a blessing and then touched them with the relic of the True Cross, which created a burning sensation on the young man and woman.[192] He then knelt down before the Blessed Sacrament and said, "Lord, what should we do?"[193] As he was praying, Fr. Benedict heard the Lord clearly say, "the Archangel."[194] Fr. Benedict then addressed the people: "We are going to pray to St. Michael the Archangel for these young people."[195] The teenagers went ballistic.

As Fr. Benedict led his team in the Chaplet of St. Michael the Archangel, the teenagers were "progressively delivered and released from the evil spirits. And by the time we finished the chaplet, they were completely released from the evil spirits."[196] The children were unconscious by the end. Fr. Benedict then secretly and quietly touched them with the relic of the True Cross, and there were no reactions. When they regained consciousness, he performed a few other tests and spoke with them privately to see if they were free and if they needed the Sacrament of Confession. This was the first exorcism Fr. Benedict had done completely with St. Michael the Archangel's intercession and only with the use of his chaplet. The children were set free in less than twenty minutes, and Fr. Benedict credits St. Michael for their liberation.[197]

---

[192] Exorcists often touch the relic of the True Cross to the possessed person as one of the key relics to help liberate the person from the grip of the demon.

[193] Fr. Benedict, in discussion with Patrick O'Hearn, December 2024.

[194] Ibid.

[195] Ibid .

[196] Ibid .

[197] Fr. Benedict also noted a providential occurrence involving St. Michael during the exorcism. After he thanked the Lord, and as he was departing from the chapel, he noticed a sizable statue of St. Michael the Archangel underneath the main altar. Fr. Benedict

St. Mary Magdalene

St. Mary Magdalene is mentioned throughout Scripture. She consoles Jesus at the foot of the Cross alongside Our Lady, and she is the first to see Jesus after His Resurrection. She knew Our Lord intimately. But she was not always a holy woman, as St. Luke mentions that Jesus' followers included "some women who had been healed of evil spirits and infirmities: Mary, called Mag'dalene, from whom seven demons had gone out" (Luke 8:2). We do not know exactly how she became possessed, but since seven is the number of perfection, it is very possible that she was actually "full of demons and completely possessed,"[198] according to Msgr. Rossetti. As a result, "she would have a special love and efficacy for those afflicted by demons."[199]

Her role in exorcisms should not be underestimated. According to Msgr. Rossetti, "We have a few 'go-to saints' who are especially powerful in exorcisms. One of these is Mary Magdalene. We especially invoke her and apply her first-class relic when the afflicted person has demons related to sexual sins. We

---

had never seen a St. Michael statue under the main altar either in that country or anywhere else in the world! And so he discovered that this little chapel, which he was visiting for the first time, was under the special protection and patronage of St. Michael. Fr. Benedict was unaware of this reality because the ten helpers surrounding the possessed person were blocking his view during the exorcism.

[198] Msgr. Stephen Rossetti, "Exorcist Diary #302: Magdalene's Powerful Presence in an Exorcism," *The St. Michael Center for Spiritual Renewal: Msgr. Rossetti's Blog,* July 28, 2024, https://www.catholic exorcism.org/post/exorcist-diary-302-magdalene-s-powerful -presence-in-an-exorcism.

[199] Ibid.

often get a strong reaction from the demons."[200] Today, in our oversexualized world, St. Mary Magdalene's role in combating the diabolical will likely intensify, as Satan seeks to drag many souls to Hell through sins of the flesh. Hence, it is not surprising that her name appears in the Litany of the Saints during the Rite of Exorcism.

While St. Mary Magdelene may often be forgotten or spoken about with less fervor compared to Our Lady, St. Joseph, St. Michael the Archangel, and other saints, she is a true warrior. She has been called the "Apostle to the Apostles" for sharing the Resurrection with the Apostles, and she might also be called the "Apostle to Exorcists," for she knows what it is like to be possessed and wants nothing more than to free souls from the bonds of the devil.

St. John the Baptist

St. John the Baptist was a sight to behold. Clad in camel skin garments, and eating locusts and wild honey, he feared no one. Even King Herod Antipas was afraid of him (see Mark 6:20). So it seems only natural that the demons would especially tremble before St. John the Baptist.

In one old exorcism ritual, the priest commands the demon to depart through the prayers and merits of the prophets and of all the saints of the Church, especially "St. John the Baptist, greater than whom was none among the men born of women."[201] Fr. Ripperger further attested to St. John the Baptist's powerful role:

---

[200] Ibid.

[201] Menghi, *The Scourge of Demons*, 100.

I did have one time during the feast of St. John the Baptist.... I invoked St. John the Baptist, and the demon just started going nuts. I'm like, "What's your problem?" and he just looks at me [and] says, "He's a big boy," referring to St. John the Baptist. By that he meant that his stature in Heaven was extraordinarily high.[202]

Indeed, Jesus' cousin was powerful while on earth, and he appears to be even more powerful now in Heaven.

St. Catherine of Siena

Another powerful ally in our battle with Satan is St. Catherine of Siena, a Third Order Dominican who lived as a virgin in her home during the fourteenth century. She led a life of intense prayer and charity, frequently visiting the sick and poor, and she ate nothing but the Eucharist for seven years. She played a pivotal role in bringing the pope back to Rome from Avignon during the Western Schism, and helped liberate the possessed during her lifetime—souls whom even the exorcists could not assist.

Fr. Ripperger related a story of St. Catherine of Siena's efficacious power against a demon:

In fact, one time there was this one demon (it was the feast of St. Catherine of Siena) and I asked St. Catherine of Siena to come down and afflict him, and he just went

---

[202] Fr. Chad Ripperger, "Fr. Ripperger's Wildest Range of Topics in One Show," September 18, 2024, Spiritual Strength with Gene Zannetti, YouTube, https://www.youtube.com/watch?v=gEKd A4xx6io&t=1942s.

bananas. Then it just kind of dawned on me and I said, "Wait a minute. You weren't the guy that got kicked out by Catherine of Siena in the public square, were you?" Then he just went crazy.[203]

During her lifetime, St. Catherine of Siena wrote inspiring letters to Church leaders, including the pope and cardinals, as well as to laypeople. These deeply spiritual letters aimed to bring about reform in the Church and encourage conversion. They also reveal her own spirituality, including self-awareness of her weaknesses and the devil's wiles, as seen in her letter to a religious man in Florence:

> I am always afraid, on account of my frailty and the astuteness of the devil, and think that I may be deceived; for I am perfectly well aware that the devil lost beatitude, but not wisdom, with which wisdom, as I said, I recognized that he might deceive me. But then I turn me, and lean against the Tree of the Most Holy Cross of Christ.[204]

St. Catherine conquered Satan through the wood of the Cross and by distrusting herself. She reminds us to place our entire trust in Jesus, for without it, we may succumb to the devil's deceptions. If we invoke her aid, she will send something far greater than a personal letter—she will intercede before the throne of God and help us overcome every temptation of the devil.

---

[203] Fr. Chad Ripperger, "Exorcisms: What Catholics Need to Know with Fr. Chad Ripperger," interview by Chris Stefanick, April 10, 2022, by Augustine Institute, YouTube.

[204] St. Catherine of Siena, *St. Catherine of Siena as Seen in Her Letters*, trans. Vida D. Scudder (New York: E. P. Dutton, 1905), 77.

Other Timeless Saints

In an exorcism, any saint has the potential to show up, though most exorcists say that often only the saints that are invoked appear. Besides the ones listed above, others who have caused powerful demonic reactions include St. Robert Bellarmine,[205] St. Joan of Arc, St. Veronica Giuliani, and St. Catherine of Bologna (a fifteenth-century Poor Clare nun).[206]

Fr. Pius adds other timeless saints as powerful allies against Satan: "I also noticed that the presence of the ancient Roman virgin martyrs, St. Agnes, St. Lucy, St. Agatha. So the ancient Virgin Martyrs seemed also to be very powerful intercessors in deliverance ministry, St. Agnes in particular."[207] Such is the power of the saints.

While many timeless saints have appeared in exorcisms, even when a demon or possessed person does not see a saint, we trust that they are involved with exorcisms. The saints were most afflicted on earth and seemed to be "punished" by men, particularly by diabolical forces working through evil people, but they now shine for all eternity, and these righteous souls are now used by God to comfort the afflicted and punish the demons. As the Book of Wisdom says:

---

[205] When asked why St. Robert Bellarmine appeared, Fr. Pius said that the possessed person may have had some knowledge of or devotion to him.

[206] Of course, Our Lady is a powerful and ready help for us as well, but she merits her own chapter and will be discussed at length later.

[207] Fr. Pius, in discussion with Patrick O'Hearn, September 2024. St. Agnes, who was brutally killed around the age of twelve or thirteen, refused every diabolical assault on earth to save herself for her spouse, Jesus.

But the souls of the righteous are in the hand of God,
and no torment will ever touch them.
In the eyes of the foolish they seemed to have died,
and their departure was thought to be an affliction,
and their going from us to be their destruction;
but they are at peace.
For though in the sight of men they were punished,
their hope is full of immortality. (3:1–4)

6

Saints of Today, Come to Our Aid

In his book *True Devotion to Mary*, St. Louis de Montfort shared a prophesy that in our present time, God would raise up "great saints who shall surpass most of the other saints in sanctity as much as the cedars of Lebanon outgrow the little shrubs."[208] These modern-day saints have proven to be extraordinarily powerful in exorcisms, as many exorcists report that several modern-day saints—those who lived in the last two centuries—are wreaking havoc on the powers of Hell and unfettering the shackles of demonic oppression and possession.

Fr. Vincent Lampert validated this point:

I think exorcists will tell you that some of the most important saints to call upon are those that we see within our own era. In the ministry of exorcism, when we invoke Mother Teresa, St. John Paul II, St. Maximilian Kolbe, and, even many exorcists tell me, the power of our new St. Carlo Acutis—if Christ is being rejected, which is ultimately what Satan has done, then invoking

<hr>

[208] St. Louis de Montfort, *True Devotion to Mary with Preparation for Total Consecration* (Charlotte, NC: Tan Books, 2010), 19.

these saints allows them to be the light that shines in the darkness.[209]

Fr. Pius explained that more and more modern-day saints are showing up in exorcisms because "they are very present in the current mentality of the Church and of Catholics. So I think that people tend to know of them and probably have some kind of a devotion to them if they're Catholic."[210]

The devil has been trying to extinguish Catholicism for over two thousand years, but the light of Christ can never be put out so long as pious souls allow the Holy Spirit to kindle the fire of God's love in them. Or in the words of Christ Himself: "I came to cast fire upon the earth; and would that it were already kindled!" (Luke 12:49). These saints set the world on fire with the love of God, driving the demons back to Hell.

St. Elena Guerra (1835–1914)

Known as the "Apostle of the Holy Spirit," St. Elena Guerra was canonized in 2024 by Pope Francis. When she was in her twenties, St. Elena was bedridden for several years, but she used her time to deepen her faith by studying the writings of the Church Fathers. Eventually, she was miraculously cured by God. Her healing inspired her to establish an order of nuns dedicated to teaching, and so she founded a religious order in Lucca, Italy, called the Oblates of the Holy Spirit, which today has houses in Italy, Cameroon, Canada, the Philippines, and Rwanda. St. Elena was a gifted writer, theologian, and teacher, and one of her most famous pupils was

---

[209] Fr. Vincent Lampert, in discussion with Patrick O'Hearn, August 2024.

[210] Fr. Pius, in discussion with Patrick O'Hearn, September 2024.

St. Gemma Galgani. Her writings were so profound that St. John Bosco once told her, "You have a pen of gold."[211]

Devoted to the Holy Spirit, St. Elena wrote several private letters to Pope Leo XIII, pleading for him to rekindle the Church's love for the Third Person of the Blessed Trinity. The Holy Father responded by asking the Church to pray a novena to the Holy Spirit between the feasts of Ascension and Pentecost, and he promoted the Holy Spirit Chaplet that St. Elena had composed. Pope Leo XIII also wrote an encyclical, *Divinum Illud Munus*, that dealt with the Holy Spirit.

Though St. Elena is not as widely known as other modern-day saints, her life has drawn the attention of at least one exorcist. After he had experienced a "long series of ugly exorcism sessions,"[212] Msgr. Rossetti kept calling upon the Holy Spirit and noticed that one demon had a "particular weakness" to this invocation.[213] In fact, the demon "howled" when the Holy Spirit was invoked.[214] Perhaps prompted by the Holy Spirit, Msgr. Rossetti and his exorcist team brought in St. Elena through the use of a first-class relic he had obtained from her order:

> In the midst of the exorcism, the team laid the first-class relic of St. Elena on the forehead on the afflicted person,

[211] Patti Mansfield, "Blessed Elena Guerra: Apostle of the Holy Spirit," *Renewal Ministries*, May 24, 2022, https://www.renewal ministries.net/blessed-elena-guerra-apostle-of-the-holy-spirit/.

[212] Msgr. Stephen Rossetti, "Exorcist Diary #324: New Saint Helps Cast Out Demon," *The St. Michael Center for Spiritual Renewal: Msgr. Rossetti's Blog*, December 28, 2024, https://www.catholic exorcism.org/post/exorcist-diary-324-new-saint-helps-cast-out-demon.

[213] Ibid.

[214] Ibid.

again and again. I have a scale of how loud the demons scream from 1 to 5. The average in an exorcism is a 3. When it hits 5, the screams are ear-splitting. When the relic was used, it went off the scale. Shortly thereafter, [the] demon finally left, thanks to the infinitely powerful Holy Spirit and the intercession of this new saint.[215]

How fitting that the "Apostle of the Holy Spirit" played a vital role in delivering this possessed soul, for the "Lord is the Spirit, and where the Spirit of the Lord is, there is freedom" (2 Cor. 3:17).

Bl. Bartolo Longo (1841–1926)[216]

Bl. Bartolo Longo was once a child of darkness. Though he was born into a devout Catholic family on February 10, 1841, after his mother died when he was ten years old, and having been pushed away from the Faith by several college professors who were ex-priests, he started to visit Naples' notorious mediums.[217] Eventually, he was sucked into the occult, and he drifted so far from the bark of St. Peter that he gave his soul to a demon and became a Satanic priest, preaching vehemently against the Church. During this time, he became very ill and psychologically unstable.

But Bartolo's family kept praying. He even heard his devout father from Heaven saying, "Return to God! Return to God!" A devout Catholic professor named Vincenzo Pepe introduced Bartolo to a Dominican priest, and Bartolo soon reverted to the

---

[215] Ibid.

[216] While we were writing this manuscript, Pope Francis approved the cause of canonization for Bl. Bartolo Longo.

[217] That is, those who try to communicate with the dead.

Faith. Still, Bartolo wrestled with major questions, and the devil was not about to let him go without a fight. He wrote:

> I recalled my former condition as a priest of Satan.... I thought that perhaps as the priesthood of Christ is for eternity, so also the priesthood of Satan is for eternity. So despite my repentance, I thought: I am still consecrated to Satan, and I am still his slave and property as he awaits me in Hell. As I pondered over my condition, I experienced a deep sense of despair and almost committed suicide. Then I heard an echo in my ear of the voice of Friar Alberto repeating the words of the Blessed Virgin Mary: "One who propagates my Rosary shall be saved." Falling to my knees, I exclaimed: "If your words are true that he who propagates your Rosary will be saved, I shall reach salvation, because I shall not leave this earth without propagating your Rosary."[218]

Bl. Bartolo then spent his life throwing out a lifeline—the Rosary—to others who might have otherwise become Satan's property. He died on October 5, 1926, in Pompeii.

When asked if Bl. Bartolo shows up in exorcism, Fr. Alphonsus stated:

> Yes, I have heard about him showing up to different exorcists. For me, one summer I was helping with a pilgrimage, and we ended up going to visit his remains. I was chosen, somehow, from among a great number of priests, randomly to be the one to celebrate Mass on the

---

[218] "A Former Satanist Priest who Became a Saint," *Dominican Friars Foundation*, https://dominicanfriars.org/former-satanist-priest -became-saint/.

altar over his body. I'd never really heard of him at that time. It was only later that one of my friends, who's an exorcist, said, "Oh, yeah, he shows up quite a bit." So I thought, oh my goodness—well, this is probably because there is a connection between Bl. Bartolo and my ministry, because it just seems like a number of possessed people, and people heavily oppressed, end up in my life without a natural explanation. I am then able to help them with spiritual direction and, ultimately, deliverance. So that's a really cool connection that I didn't even understand when I offered Mass at the altar over his body.[219]

Other exorcists such as Fr. Athanasius invoke Bl. Bartolo Longo frequently and promote his cultus, but they report that so far, they have only gotten "minimal reactions in the screamometer."[220] Still, we can rest assured that this saintly man, who knew the devil well during life, is now a powerful and keen ally from Heaven.

St. Mary of Jesus Crucified (1846–1878)

After losing their first twelve children (all boys) in infancy, a faithful Melkite Catholic couple made a pilgrimage to Bethlehem, where they pleaded to Our Lady for a daughter, whom they would name Mariam. And so Mariam Baouardy was born on January 5, 1846, near Nazareth. Yet from infancy on, God would lead Mariam down the path of Calvary. Her parents died when she was only three years old, and Mariam was adopted by her uncle. When Mariam

---

[219] Fr. Alphonsus, in discussion with Charles D. Fraune, August 2024

[220] Fr. Athanasius, in discussion with Charles D. Fraune, October 2024. The "screamometer" is a term given by Fr. Athanasius that refers to how much a demon will scream at a certain saint's name.

was nearly thirteen, her uncle arranged for her to marry his wife's brother, but after she declined, he grew angry and forced her to work as a servant in the kitchens. Soon after, she was approached by a Muslim man who wanted her to convert to Islam and marry him. When she refused, he slit her throat and left her for dead. Yet Mariam lived: she reported that a nun in blue had cared for her and told her that she would become a nun herself. Mariam later believed that this nun had really been Our Lady.[221]

Mariam eventually entered religious life at the age of nineteen, yet she was dismissed by the first community she joined after they failed to understand her mystical gifts. She then entered the Carmelite Order in Pao, France, and she eventually was led to found a Carmel in Bethlehem just three years before her death in 1878. She suffered greatly during life, as in addition to her worldly troubles, she was also tormented by demons and possessed at least twice.[222]

While the sufferings a saint experiences in life serve to perfect them into saints, their battle scars are not just for themselves but also for us today, as God continues to use the saints' victories and defeats as the means to assist those who are facing demonic attacks, temptations, and possession. St. Mary of Jesus Crucified suffered for her faith in the Muslim Middle East, and she dealt with her own demonic struggles. And so as the persecution of Catholics intensifies worldwide, especially in the Middle East, St. Mary of Jesus Crucified—who was once possessed and nearly became a martyr—will likely have an even greater intercessory role.

---

[221] "Saint Mary of Jesus Crucified," *Carmelite Sisters of Ireland*, February 11, 2025, https://www.carmelitesisters.ie/blessed-mary-of-jesus-crucified-miriam-baouardy/.

[222] Rossetti, *Diary of an American Exorcist*, 208.

St. Thérèse of Lisieux (1878–1897)

As the youngest child of two saintly parents, Sts. Louis and Zélie Martin, St. Thérèse of Lisieux had two of the greatest models for holiness. One of her nicknames, which she gave herself, was the "little flower," as she was content to be a little flower in God's garden. But far from being a tiny, helpless flower, she was one of the devil's fiercest opponents, for she lived entirely for God and longed to save as many souls as possible through her prayers and penance. As a result, the devil pursued her constantly throughout her twenty-four years of life.

In her autobiography, *The Story of a Soul*, St. Thérèse described a vivid and disturbing dream she had around the age of three or four. She wrote,

> I was walking alone in the garden when suddenly I saw two horrible little devils near the arbor, dancing on a barrel of lime with amazing agility, in spite of having heavy irons on their feet. They looked at me with flaming eyes, then, as if overcome by fear, threw themselves in the twinkling of an eye to the bottom of the barrel. They escaped in some mysterious way and ran off to hide in the linen room, which opens onto the garden. When I saw how cowardly they were, I put my fears aside and went over to the window to see what they were up to. There the little wretches were, running round and round the table, and not knowing how to escape my gaze. From time to time they came nearer, still very agitated, to peep through the window; then, when they saw I was still there, they began racing about again in abject misery.
>
> I do not suppose this dream was very extraordinary, but I do think God made use of it to show me that a soul

in the state of grace need never be afraid of the devil, who is such a coward that even the gaze of a child will frighten him away.[223]

The attacks only intensified throughout her life. During a childhood illness, the devil assailed her openly. On the eve of her vows as a Carmelite nun, he sowed seeds of doubt, making her feel "quite unsuited"[224] for religious life. Near the end of her life, as she battled tuberculosis, she sensed the devil's presence in her cell: "I do not see him, but I feel him near me. He crucifies me in a grip of iron to deprive me of all consolation, trying, by increasing my sufferings, to make me despair."[225] To banish the devil, St. Thérèse kept her eyes on Our Lady and repeated the holy Name of Jesus while keeping a blessed candle lit.[226] She also sometimes relied on holy water to drive the devil away.[227]

Because of her lifelong battles and triumphs over the ancient serpent, St. Thérèse longs to assist those who invoke her intercession today. Fr. Benedict recalled one story when he prayed over a young man at a United States shrine who roared like a lion, which "scared people to death."[228] Some people even cried. Fr. Benedict assured the people not to worry and that God would take care of setting the man free. The young man was taken to an outside room, and Fr. Benedict obtained permission from the bishop of that diocese to perform an exorcism. As soon as the

[223] St. Thérèse of Lisieux, *The Story of a Soul*, 12–13.
[224] Ibid, 98.
[225] Ibid., 173.
[226] Ibid.
[227] Ibid.
[228] Fr. Benedict, in discussion with Patrick O'Hearn, December 2024.

Exorcism Ritual started, the young man fell into a comatose state. Fr. Benedict then noticed that those helping him were tired. This was an unplanned exorcism, and it was already late at night. Fr. Benedict recognized that the devil would want this exorcism to go on all night, so he looked up to Heaven and said, "Jesus, my people are worn out. This is going to take a long time. Could you give me a shortcut so they could go home?" He continued:

> Immediately, the thought came to me. A thought from the Holy Spirit: St. Thérèse. It was like a spoken command in my soul. It was an answer. I looked up and said "What?" Because as an exorcist, I have never been trained to call upon St. Thérèse. She's a little twenty-four-year-old nun … a little girl. What could she do here? This is one of the most powerful demonic manifestations I have ever seen.[229]

But the Lord again told Fr. Benedict, "Thérèse." So he began to pray the Chaplet of St. Thérèse, praying twenty-four Glory Be's to the Little Flower. The man was instantaneously set free and woke up after the seventh Glory Be.

Sometimes, when St. Thérèse of Lisieux shows up in an exorcism, she does not come alone. According to Adam Blai, "her parents now go with her."[230] Sts. Louis and Zélie Martin fight side by side with their saintly daughter like their own "little holy family."

St. Gemma Galgani (1878–1903)

Born on March 12, 1878, in Italy—just three months after St. Thérèse—St. Gemma Galgani lived a brief but holy life. She

---

[229] Ibid.
[230] Adam Blai, in discussion with Patrick O'Hearn, October 2024.

became a third order Passionists after poor health prevented her from becoming a nun, had many mystical experiences, including receiving the stigmata (the wounds of Christ), and fought the devil throughout her life. She was even physically beaten by the devil. As St. Gemma related, "Once more I have passed a bad night. The demon came before me as a giant of great height. He beat me fiercely all night and kept saying to me: 'For thee there is no more hope of salvation. Thou art in my hands.'"[231] The devil continued to assault St. Gemma, but her trust in God and her lack of fear only infuriated him, so he dragged her from her bed and slammed her head against the floor. But St. Gemma stayed firm in her faith. Today she is one of the patron saints against temptations.

Now this saint whom God allowed to be beaten by Satan beats the ancient dragon to a pulp. For "God chose what is foolish in the world to shame the wise, God chose what is weak in the world to shame the strong" (1 Cor. 1:27).

Msgr. Rossetti once shared a powerful story regarding St. Gemma and a young woman named Valerie who had been immersed in the occult for ten years. After Valerie tried to break free, demons attacked her daily. Weekly deliverance sessions, which lasted a full year, helped loosen Satan's grip, and during this time, Valerie once dreamed of St. Gemma's Shrine in Italy, though she had never heard of St. Gemma. She also said that "whenever she sees a picture of beautiful Gemma and prays for her help, the demons react strongly. She said they 'hate' her and have a 'pure disgust' for her. The demons tormenting Valerie

---

[231] Ven. Fr. Germanus, C.P., *The Life of St. Gemma Galgani*, trans. Fr. A. M. O'Sullivan (Charlotte, NC: Tan Books, 2012), 189.

make her feel like 'vomiting' whenever St. Gemma is invoked. They shout, 'Keep that woman away from me!' "[232]

Dave VanVickle, who assists priests with exorcisms, also related a story about St. Gemma:

One day, I was doing an intake for a diocese. It was an eighteen-year-old kid, sitting between his two uncles, who were firefighters. They were these huge guys, and he was just foaming at the mouth and screaming obscenities when they brought him into my office. They sat down on the couch, probably like twenty feet away from me from where I was sitting behind my desk. He calmed down a little bit and I started asking him questions; just normal questions, like, "Well, how do you do in school? Do you play any sports?" Things like that. At one point I said, "Joshua [pseudonym], do you know how much God loves you?" Then all of a sudden, his eyes, like, rolled back in his head, and before I could even blink, he had broken this vase and had come and placed it up against my throat. It had to have been less than a second that he had this vase up against my throat. I thought, "Oh my gosh, he's going to kill me." He looked above me, stopped, and he looked at me and said, "If that little dago[233] from Lucca weren't behind you, I'd have killed you three seconds ago." I had no idea who this was! I was like, "What is he talking about?" and he

---

[232] Msgr. Stephen Rossetti, "Exorcist Diary #176: Demons Hate Gemma," *The St. Michael Center for Spiritual Renewal: Msgr. Rossetti's Blog*, February 5, 2022, https://www.catholicexorcism.org/post/exorcist-diary-176-demons-hate-gemma.

[233] "Dago" is a derogatory term for a person of Italian or Spanish birth or descent.

just sat down real gently and kept looking up and kind of behind me, as if to see what was going on behind me. This kid was eventually admitted for exorcism, and every time I would walk in, the demon would start talking about this "little girl from Lucca." Finally, the exorcist demanded to know who it was: it was St. Gemma Galgani.[234]

Fr. Pius also noted that "St. Gemma Galgani is also a very, very powerful intercessor, and the demons would react strongly to her intercession."[235] The demons often refer to St. Gemma Galgani as "that one dressed in black,"[236]and among all the saints that show up in exorcisms, she is the fourth most popular after St. Teresa of Calcutta, Pope St. John Paul II, and St. Rita of Cascia.[237]

And so St. Gemma, who suffered greatly at the hands of the enemy during her life, now stands on the front lines in the fight against Satan. The serpent has become, once again, the means of his own undoing. As the Lord told St. Gemma, "Be prepared, My child. The devil, at My bidding, shall be the one who, by the war he will wage against thee, will give the last touch to the work that I will accomplish in thee."[238]

St. Padre Pio (1887–1968)

Another Italian saint who terrifies Satan is St. Padre Pio. Born on May 25, 1887, just nine years after St. Gemma, he too experienced

---

[234] Dave VanVickle, *Truth and Shadow Podcast*, episode 25.

[235] Fr. Pius, in discussion with Patrick O'Hearn, September 2024.

[236] Fr. Francesco Bamonte, *The Virgin Mary and the Devil in Exorcisms* (Milan, Italy: Paoline, 2014), 167.

[237] Fr. Timothy, in discussion with Charles D. Fraune, August 2024.

[238] Germanus, *The Life of St. Gemma Galgani*, 183.

his share of demonic attacks. The devil would often beat him with heavy chains, leaving him bruised and bloody, or appear to him under the guise of hideous animals, nude women, his superiors, or even as holy people like Jesus or Mary.

Fr. Amorth was one of St. Padre Pio's spiritual sons and faithfully visited him every year for twenty-six years. He noted that Pio never performed official exorcisms and was not an official exorcist, yet

> Padre Pio was given a special grace to discern whether demoniacs were "mature" enough to be liberated from their demons. When he encountered a demoniac whose moment of liberation (as appointed by God) had not yet come, he would give her a blessing and send her on her way. There was nothing else he could do, because all his power came from God. Conversely, some of the worst cases of possession can be "cured" almost instantaneously. Padre Pio was also known to speak a few words to a demoniac ("Go away from him!"), and the demon would instantly depart.[239]

For example, St. Padre Pio helped liberate a possessed teenage girl from Bergamo whom a few Capuchins had failed to free. Pio spent the entire night in prayer after learning about the unsuccessful exorcism and was then brutally assaulted by the devil. A few days later, he regained his strength to celebrate Mass. The possessed girl was in the congregation, and when she saw Pio, she shrieked and then passed out. A few minutes later, when the girl awoke, the devil had left her. She attended Mass immediately after she was liberated.[240]

---

[239] Amorth, *The Pope's Exorcist*, 67–68.

[240] Alberto D'Apolito, *Padre Pio of Pietrelcina: Memories, Experiences, Testimonials* (Edizioni Padre Pio da Pietrelcina, 2013), 99–102.

After St. Padre Pio died, Fr. Amorth began to experience his strong assistance in exorcisms: "Padre Pio died in '68, and I was nominated in '86. Yet he was close to me when I needed him! At various times, during the exorcisms, the demon would say, through the person being exorcised: 'Away with that priest. I do not want him!'" [241] Other exorcists have also stated how much the demons hate St. Padre Pio and how invoking his name causes a great reaction. Fr. Ripperger, who was once asked which saints, besides Our Lady, St. Joseph, and St. Michael the Archangel, have given him direct assistance in an exorcism, explained:

> The one that [I see] probably the most is Padre Pio. My nickname for him is "Johnny on the spot," because you just ask him to show up and, boom, he's right there. I think it's God's way of giving him satisfaction for having been beat up by demons in this life; they get their come-uppance. In fact, it's so funny, it's kind of extraordinary; one time, with this one woman, the demon would not sit still so I just turned to Padre Pio, and I said, "Would you get this guy under control," and all of a sudden, the woman just goes, *wham*, down on the ground and writhing around. Afterwards, I asked her what happened. She said, "I don't know, but I could feel his foot on my back!"[242]

St. Maria Goretti (1890–1902)

One of the most powerful saints of our times is St. Maria Goretti, the patron saint of youth, young women, purity, and victims of rape.

[241] Amorth, *My Battle against Satan*, 25.
[242] Ripperger, "Our Lady of Sorrows and Healing."

On July 6, 1902, Maria was approached by twenty-year-old Alessandro Serenelli, who was nearly mad with a diabolical desire for Maria's precious gift of virginity. Alessandro threatened to kill her if she refused him. Faced with an unimaginable choice, Maria nevertheless stood firm in her purity. As Fr. Godfrey Poage, C.P., asserted:

> The knife now hangs over her breast. She must choose death or life, Heaven or Hell, God or Satan, sin or martyrdom. In a burst of heroism, making desperate efforts to free herself, she chooses energetically, superhumanly.
>
> "No! No! It is a sin! God does not want this! If you do this, you will go to Hell! What are you doing, Alessandro! You will go to Hell!"[243]

St. Maria Goretti was more concerned for her attacker's salvation than for her own life—such is the beauty of this saint. As Alessandro stabbed her fourteen times, she "tried to hold her dress modestly over her knees"[244] before losing consciousness. She finally succumbed to her wounds and died. She was just eleven years old. Truly, St. Maria Goretti was both a virgin martyr and a martyr of modesty.

As immodesty, pornography, and sexual perversion continue to escalate in our time, St. Maria Goretti's role in the battle for purity has become even more pronounced. In particular, Fr. Szada has spoken of her strong presence in exorcisms: "The one I could think of would be St. Maria Goretti. She'd be very powerful these days especially with the catastrophe we have in terms of sexual sins and all that stuff. She tends to be very, very powerful."[245]

---

[243] Fr. Godfrey Poage, C.P., *St. Maria Goretti: In Garments All Red* (Charlotte, NC: TAN Books, 2012), 37.

[244] Ibid., 38.

[245] Fr. John Szada, in discussion with Patrick O'Hearn, August 2024.

St. Maximilian Kolbe (1894–1941)

Born in Poland in 1894, St. Maximilian Kolbe is another dragon slayer. After he was arrested by Nazis in 1941, he suffered ruthlessly in a concentration camp and ultimately offered his own life in the place of a married man named Franciszek Gajowniczek. He survived two weeks without food and water, leading the others sentenced to death in prayer each day, but the Nazis finally killed St. Maximilian Kolbe and the other surviving inmates by injecting them with carbolic acid.

Well before he offered his life for God and his brother, St. Maximilian Kolbe was snatching souls for Christ through his beloved "Immaculata" (his term for Mary).

His Catholic publication press inspired millions of people to deepen their faith and consecrate their lives to the Blessed Virgin Mary and boldly defended the Church against its enemies of the time, especially the Freemasons and the Nazis. Furthermore, he worked to save refugees from the Nazi regime and sheltered as many as two thousand Jews in his monastery. While many lamented that new modes of media technology were in the possession of Satan, St. Maximilian Kolbe saw an opportunity to win souls for Christ: "Souls are being lost, Satan multiplies his conquests, and the atheistic press prospers.... All the more reason to finally wake up and get to work in order to reconquer the positions taken by the enemy."[246] As he said, "Our purpose is to conquer for Christ, to win all the world and all souls without exception for the Immaculate—never material gain."[247] And conquer St. Maximilian did.

---

[246] Maria Winowska, *Our Lady's Fool: Father Maximilian Kolbe*, trans. Therese Plumereau (Westminster, MD: The Newman Press, 1952), 94, 44.

[247] Ibid., 94.

Perhaps it was for these reasons that Fr. Vincent Lampert believed that St. Maximilian Kolbe is one of the most powerful saints in exorcisms,[248] for those who sought to conquer the world for Christ on earth continue to do so in Heaven. Indeed, as more and more souls are joining the occult and other anti-Catholic groups like the Freemasons, St. Maximilian Kolbe's role in exorcism could be even greater.

St. Teresa of Calcutta (1910–1997)

St. Teresa of Calcutta was around five feet tall, though while she was small in stature, she was a force to be reckoned with. She was born on August 26, 1910, in Skopje, in northern Macedonia, and she devoted her life to helping the poor and the forsaken, including the unborn, as she once told world leaders in her acceptance speech for the Noble Peace Prize in 1979, "The greatest destroyer of peace today is the cry of the innocent unborn child."[249] She was a woman of deep prayer who especially adored Jesus in the Holy Eucharist, and she helped snatch many souls for Christ's Kingdom. St. Teresa of Calcutta knew the struggle between good and evil and spent her life committed to God's service as a religious sister and the founder of the Missionaries of Charity. Therefore, the devil had much to fear from this tiny but mighty woman. She also endured the dark night of the soul for nearly fifty years, suffering profound spiritual dryness without interior consolation.

[248] Fr. Vincent Lampert, in discussion with Patrick O'Hearn, August 2024.

[249] "Mother Teresa Acceptance Speech," The Nobel Prize, December 10, 1979, https://www.nobelprize.org/prizes/peace/1979/teresa /acceptance-speech/.

In addition to her own work saving souls for Christ and helping the poor and suffering of India, St. Teresa also experienced a demonic attack herself shortly before her death on September 5, 1997. Archbishop Henry Sebastian D'Souza of Calcutta witnessed the incident:

> She and I were in the same hospital when I noticed she got very agitated at night although she was very peaceful during the day. When there was no medical explanation for it, I concluded it could be the tag of the devil.... I then asked a priest to perform an exorcism prayer on her. It lasted for half-an-hour.[250]

After the exorcism, Mother Teresa was relieved from her agitation and was able to sleep peacefully through the night.

Throughout her life, St. Teresa of Calcutta faced many spiritual battles. Her steadfastness to Christ amid these trials, including the demonic attack before her death and deep spiritual desolation, became a catalyst for her sanctity. Now, in eternity, she intercedes for those who seek her help, especially in times of spiritual warfare, dryness, and even possession. As Fr. Bamonte recalled:

> At the beginning of the exorcism, I prayed the Litany of the Saints, during which I invoked St. Gemma Galgani, Blessed Mother Theresa of Calcutta, and the Servant of God, Pope John Paul II.[251] A few minutes later, the demon

---

[250] "Mother Teresa Felt 'Tag of the Devil,'" *The Irish Times*, September 7, 2001, https://www.irishtimes.com/news/mother-teresa-felt-tag-of-the-devil-1.326164.

[251] This account was first published in 2010. Pope Francis canonized St. Teresa of Calcutta in 2016 and Pope St. John Paul II in 2014.

said, "That one dressed in black like you arrived." The demon was referring to St. Gemma Galgani, who often intervenes to help exorcists and possessed persons who pray to her. The demon exclaimed, "The Albanian also arrived, that little one!"[252] in reference to Blessed Mother Theresa of Calcutta, whose intercession I asked for in the litany. Soon thereafter, the demon added, "Oh look at them! Look at them! They are hugging. They are greeting each other, those two stupid people! How disgusting! How disgusting!"[253]

Later in that same exorcism, Fr. Bamonte and his team prayed intensely on their knees. Suddenly, the demon exclaimed, "No, nooo, even these others have gotten on their knees: that white one (referring to John Paul II), that black one (referring to St. Gemma Galgani), that little white one (referring to Blessed Mother Teresa of Calcutta), and her [Mary]."[254] With such holy companions, St. Teresa of Calcutta shows us that she is indeed part of a mighty army in the fight against Satan.

Pope St. John Paul II (1920–2005)

Karol Wojtyla Jr. was a true saint of God who not only kept his faith throughout a lifetime of suffering but also helped to win millions of souls for Christ. He was born on May 18, 1920, in

---

[252] St. Teresa of Calcutta is of Albanian descent.

[253] Fr. Francesco Bamonte, *The Virgin Mary and the Devil in Exorcisms*, 167–168.

[254] Ibid. Fr. Bamonte also noted that "the demon said the pronoun 'she' to refer to Our Lady with a tone of voice that revealed fear but also unavoidable reverence and admiration at the same time."

Poland. By the time he was twenty, Karol had lost not only his parents but also his older brother, with whom he had been very close. He lived through the evils of World War II, witnessed the horrors of Nazi and Communist persecutions in eastern Europe, and personally suffered from frail health after two failed assassination attempts. And we cannot imagine the burden and sufferings he bore as he led the Church as the Supreme Pontiff for nearly twenty-seven years. Pope St. John Paul II truly knew Christ Crucified.

He also gave the devil many reasons to hate him. He was ordained to the priesthood on November 1, 1946, the Feast of All Saints, became a bishop in 1958, and served as pope from 1978 until his death in 2005. Through his clarity of teaching, especially on matters of sexual morality, he built a culture of life and drew millions of young people to the Holy Eucharist and Our Lady. He was a fisher of men who sought to convert as many as possible, and he inspired the world through his selfless love and leadership. He was also instrumental in ending the evils of communism in eastern Europe.

In addition to Pope St. John Paul II's personal sufferings, which strengthened his resolve and his faith, as well as his active work for God's Kingdom while he was alive, he also performed several exorcisms himself, although he was not a formal exorcist. We already recounted one story of Pope St. John Paul II performing an exorcism on a possessed woman while he was pope in the introduction of this book, and according to Fr. Amorth, he performed at least three such exorcisms during his papacy.[255]

Because Pope St. John Paul II was such a fierce enemy of the devil while he was alive, it should come as no surprise that his

---

[255] Amorth, *An Exorcist Explains the Demonic*, 126.

prayers and presence have proven to be especially powerful in exorcisms now. Indeed, according to many exorcists, he is one of the most frequent saints who appears in exorcisms. Fr. Pius called him a "very powerful intercessor" and said that "the demons hate him and hate his invocation."[256] Fr. Amorth noticed that an image of Pope St. John Paul II was "particularly efficacious [in exorcisms], because the demons become very irritable before him."[257] Fr. Bamonte added that during one exorcism, the demon began to scream, "Nooooo! *Totus Tuus* arrived! No, go away. Don't touch me. Go away!"[258]

St. Carlo Acutis (1991–2006)

St. Carlo Acutis will be the first "millennial" to be canonized.[259] His love for the Holy Eucharist and his desire to spread devotion via his exhibition of Eucharistic miracles has touched many lives, and his life story shows us that twenty-first century Catholics have some big, saintly shoes to fill.

Born on May 3, 1991, St. Carlo Acutis was a friend of the saints. He loved praying at their tombs, and he had a deep love for St. Francis of Assisi, St. Anthony of Padua, St. Dominic Savio, St. Bernadette, St. Padre Pio, St. Gemma Galgani, and the three

---

[256] Fr. Pius, in discussion with Patrick O'Hearn, September 2024.

[257] Amorth and Stanzione, *The Devil Is Afraid of Me*, 11.

[258] Bamonte, *The Virgin Mary and the Devil in Exorcisms*, 168. *Totus Tuus* was Pope St. John Paul II's personal motto, meaning "totally yours" and referring to his total consecration to the Blessed Mother.

[259] A "millennial" is anyone born between 1981 and 1996. At the time this manuscript was written, Carlo Acutis's canonization had been scheduled but had not yet occurred. Regardless, we call him "St. Carlo Acutis" throughout this book.

Fatima visionaries. He loved visiting Assisi so much that his family purchased a home there.

To understand the devil's hatred for St. Carlo Acutis, we only need to look at what God accomplished through him. While the devil seeks to extinguish the flame of God's love in all people, St. Carlo was a light, always encouraging others to attend Mass, always helping the poor, always standing up for the unborn and his bullied classmates.

In terms of his role in exorcisms, St. Carlo Acutis's impact is only starting. Fr. Lampert recounted one exorcism in which Carlo Acutis's name was invoked and "the demon just went completely ballistic."[260] Fr. Benedict also testified to St. Carlo Acutis's powerful intercession. "I've seen reactions when I call on him in prayer for people. I do see reactions from the evil spirit."[261]

Fr. Timothy is also seeing St. Carlo Acutis's power in exorcisms:

> It's crazy how Carlo is already there and we're already calling out to Carlo. It helps that I've been going to Carlo's tomb in Assisi for a couple of years, and it's so much fun to know he's so active that I'll say to my new Don Carlo, "Come with me now. We're going to purify, and do a deep scrub, of these cell phones that have been used in a pornographic way." Even yesterday, I was blessing three cell phones that had been used in impure ways because I get demonic messages at 3:00 a.m. The demonic messages are blocked when I bless cell phones, and I use the

---

[260] Fr. Vincent Lampert, in discussion with Patrick O'Hearn, August 2024.

[261] Fr. Benedict has not been doing exorcisms recently, so it will be interesting to see how St. Carlo Acutis's impact plays out in the future.

intercession of, as we now understand him, the patron saint of "all things internet," Carlo Acutis.[262]

St. Carlo Acutis only used technology, especially the internet, for good. The Vatican examined his entire internet search history for his beatification process and found that every search involved something for the Faith.[263] As a result, St. Carlo Acutis could play a powerful role in helping people fight pornographic temptations as well as those who are now afflicted or even possessed because of impure images. Msgr. Rossetti once said that "a pornography addiction, like any serious sin, is an opening to the demonic."[264] Hence, St. Carlo Acutis can be invoked to help those who have become possessed due to pornography or technology addiction.

Today, as more and more saints are beatified and canonized, exorcists have an ever-growing pool of heavenly allies to call upon. These saints chose to serve God over the world and continue to help us fight against Satan and all his evil forces. While the saying goes that "the devil has no knees"[265] and refuses to kneel before

---

[262] Fr. Timothy, in discussion with Charles D. Fraune, August 2024.

[263] Sabrina Arena Ferrisi, *Blessed Carlo Acutis: The Amazing Discovery of a Teenager in Heaven* (Cramerton, NC: Holy Heroes Books, 2022), 45.

[264] Joe Bukuras, "Exorcist Says Porn Addiction 'An Opening to the Demonic,' Despite German Priest's Controversial Denials," *Catholic News Agency*, December 1, 2022, https://www.catholicnewsagency .com/news/252967/exorcist-says-porn-addiction-an-opening-to -the-demonic-despite-german-priest-s-controversial-denials.

[265] Quotation attributed to the Desert Father Abba Apollo. See Bishop Thomas J. Olmstead, "Knees to Love Christ," *Catholic Culture*, https://www.catholicculture.org/culture/library/view. cfm?recnum=6378. On this note, Fr. Benedict once described an exorcism that occurred in Central America involving a teenage boy who tried to commit a murder. The boy had come in contact

almighty God, the saints spent countless hours on their knees adoring their Eucharistic Lord in the chapel or in the hiddenness of their cell. Indeed, had we been blessed to see certain saints' kneecaps, we would be astonished at how worn down they were by their prayers! Now their kneeling continues as they beg Almighty God to free those who are possessed.

with a Satanic cult in the United States over the internet. One of the instructions from the Satanic cult was to commit a specific kind of murder. The merciful judge said he would release the boy to his parents under one condition: that he would be brought to Fr. Benedict for an exorcism. Fr. Benedict brought the family into his adoration chapel and had the family pray the Rosary with him. Fr. Benedict then began to bless every family member with oil. Each of the family members knelt down, but the devil would not allow the teenage boy to kneel. Fr. Benedict added that the "devil will not kneel, and those he possesses cannot kneel either. He won't let them."

7

Our Lady Slams Satan's Door

While all of the timeless and modern-day saints are truly power-ful, there is one person whom the devil fears more than all of the saints combined, a person who makes the demons weep in terror. This person is, of course, Our Lady, Mary, the Mother of God. As Fr. Benedict said, "The number one saint is the Virgin Mary. It would be very, very foolish for a priest to enter an exor-cism without the Virgin Mary at his side."[266]

It is no coincidence that the two bookends of Scripture—Gen-esis and Revelation—allude to Our Lady's powerful role in Salva-tion History. In Genesis 3:15, known as the Protoevangelium,[267] God says to the serpent, "I will put enmity between you and the woman, and between your seed and her seed; he shall bruise your head, and you shall bruise his heel,"[268] promising that through the

---

[266] Fr. Benedict, in discussion with Patrick O'Hearn, December 2024.

[267] The Protoevangelium is the first declaration of God's planned salvation of humanity. Many saints believe that the "woman" refers to Mary.

[268] The Latin text of Genesis 3:15 from the Vulgate Bible translates to "She will crush your head." While newer translations, based on the original Hebrew, have "he," the Douay-Rheims Bible has

woman and her seed, sin and evil would be conquered. Indeed, Our Lady is the New Eve. While Eve grasped for the fruit of the tree, Mary offered the fruit of her womb upon a Tree. Jesus Himself draws the connection between His holy mother and Eve, "the mother of all living" (Gen. 3:20), when he calls her "Woman" at Cana and at Calvary (see John 2:4 and John 19:26), just as Adam named his new companion "woman" in Genesis 2:23.

The Book of Revelation describes the ongoing battle between Satan and humanity, particularly as it pertains to the diabolical assault on the New Adam, Jesus,[269] and the New Eve, Mary:

> And a great portent appeared in heaven, a woman clothed with the sun, with the moon under her feet, and on her head a crown of twelve stars; she was with child and she cried out in her pangs of birth, in anguish for delivery. And another portent appeared in heaven; behold, a great red dragon, with seven heads and ten horns, and seven diadems upon his heads. His tail swept down a third of the stars of heaven, and cast them to the earth. And the

---

"she," based on the Vulgate. This Latin version has also inspired many statues and paintings of Our Lady crushing the ancient serpent's head with her foot. As St. Alphonsus Liguori clarified, "However that may be, it is certain that either the Son (by means of His mother) or the mother (by virtue of the Son) has defeated Lucifer" (quoted in Fr. Francesco Bamonte, *The Virgin Mary and the Devil in Exorcisms*, 25).

[269] The Church's teaching that Jesus is the New Adam originates from St. Paul's comparison of Adam to Jesus in which he showed that Christ's *obedience* canceled Adam's *disobedience* (Rom. 5:19). Jesus becomes "the last Adam" who is "a life-giving spirit." He adds, "The first man was from the earth, a man of dust; the second man is from heaven" (1 Cor. 15:45–47).

dragon stood before the woman who was about to bear a child, that he might devour her child when she brought it forth; she brought forth a male child, one who is to rule all the nations with a rod of iron, but her child was caught up to God and to his throne, and the woman fled into the wilderness, where she has a place prepared by God. (12:1–6)

This ancient dragon still seeks to devour us, just as he sought to devour Our Lady and her Son in the Book of Revelation. As St. Peter warns us, "Be sober, be watchful. Your adversary the devil prowls around like a roaring lion, seeking someone to devour" (1 Pet. 5:8). But Our Lady is more powerful than all of Hell. As St. Bernard of Clairvaux declared, "the Evil One is always compelled to obey the commands of the Queen like someone who has lost the war and has become a slave."[270] She is the greatest of mothers, the Virgin most powerful, and our constant ally in our fight against evil.

After all, God chose His Mother to play a pivotal role in His work of redemption as well as in our own redemption. As Pope St. John Paul II wrote, "For Mary, present in the Church as the Mother of the Redeemer, takes part, as a mother, in that monumental struggle against the powers of darkness which continues throughout human history."[271] Our Lady came to undo the knot that was tied by Eve in the garden, and her instrumental role in Salvation History will continue until the end of time, until the last soul is born and saved.

---

[270] Bamonte, *The Virgin Mary and the Devil in Exorcisms*, 25.

[271] Pope St. John Paul II, encyclical letter *Redemptoris Mater* (March 25, 1987), no. 47.

Why the Devil Hates and Fears Mary

Because only a pure vessel could hold God in her blessed womb, God bestowed upon Mary the singular privilege of being preserved from Original Sin, which means she was completely free from the devil's clutches. Mary is the untainted handmaid of the Lord, and her Immaculate Conception makes her fearsome and loathsome to the demons.

The devil hates Our Lady because the devil hates everything about God, especially anything pertaining to the Incarnation. Every time the devil sees Mary, he is reminded of God's infinite love for humanity and how God raised human nature above the angels.[272] Fr. Bamonte explained, "The demons have an irrepressible and venomous hate for Mary. They would like to annihilate her if they could. For this reason, they oppose her actions, and they consider her the woman who is destroying their empire."[273]

What specifically does the devil hate about Our Lady? For one, she is his exact opposite. Fr. Lampert avowed that Our Lady "is the most powerful ally. She's the Queen of Heaven, the Queen of

[272] As Pope St. Leo the Great wrote, "[At the Ascension], in the sight of the holy multitude, above the dignity of all heavenly creatures, the Nature of mankind went up, to pass above the angels' ranks and to rise beyond the archangels' heights, and to have Its uplifting limited by no elevation until, received to sit with the Eternal Father, It should be associated on the throne with His glory, to Whose Nature It was united in the Son" (Pope St. Leo the Great, "Sermon 73," no. 4, in *Nicene and Post-Nicene Fathers, Second Series*, vol. 12, trans. Charles Lett Feltoe, ed. Philip Schaff and Henry Wace (Buffalo, NY: Christian Literature Publishing Co., 1895); rev. and ed. Kevin Knight, http://www.newadvent .org/fathers/360373.htm).

[273] Bamonte, *The Virgin Mary and the Devil in Exorcisms*, 14.

the Angels, and she's also the Queen of the Saints. What virtue does she bring to the battle? Humility."[274] Compare the humility of the Virgin, who said, "Behold, I am the handmaid of the Lord; let it be to me according to your word" (Luke 1:38), to the pride of the devil, of whom Scripture says:

> You said in your heart, "I will ascend to heaven; above the stars of God I will set my throne on high; I will sit on the mount of assembly in the far north; I will ascend above the heights of the clouds, I will make myself like the Most High." But you are brought down to Sheol, to the depths of the Pit. (Isa. 14:13–15)

The proud Satan is no match for the humble Virgin, for "Pride goes before destruction, and a haughty spirit before a fall" (Prov. 16:18), but "The reward for humility and fear of the Lord is riches and honor and life" (Prov. 22:4).

The demons also hate the very name of Mary. While we know that the Name of Jesus has authority, as Scripture declares, "At the name of Jesus every knee should bow, in heaven and on earth and under the earth, and every tongue confess that Jesus Christ is Lord, to the glory of God the Father" (Phil. 2:10–11), the name of Mary causes demons intense pain: "They shriek, they scream, they become more timid, they become more agitated" at the name of Mary, declared Fr. Lampert. The demons even refuse to say her name, referring to her as "that woman."[275] Fr. Pius also affirmed that Mary's name has a distinct effect on the demons compared to Jesus' name: "This power is different from

---

[274] Fr. Vincent Lampert, in discussion with Patrick O'Hearn, August 2024.
[275] Rossetti, *Diary of an American Exorcist*, 123.

the way the name of Jesus has power over them; the name of Mary is more of a humiliation, whereas the name of Jesus seems to be more of an authoritative power of command."[276] Certain titles of Mary are particularly powerful, such as Mother of God or the Immaculate Conception. In fact, Fr. Lampert stated that the title "Mary, Mother of God" is the most powerful Marian title because it testifies to the reason behind Satan's fall: the rejection of the Incarnation.[277] Perhaps this is one of the main reasons the Church places the name of Mary first in the Litany of the Saints: the Catholic Church and her saints know how mighty the name of Mary is.

Fr. Ripperger once pressed Beelzebub, the prince of demons, and another name for Satan, what was it about Our Lady that he did not like. Beelzebub replied, "It was the fact that when she (Our Lady) sacrificed herself to God, she never once counted the personal cost."[278] In other words, Our Lady never thought about herself. She lived entirely for God, always saying yes to His plan. This sacrificial spirit makes her powerful and at the same time despised by the demons. For although Our Lady was conceived without sin, her life was filled with the greatest sufferings, trials, and temptations. Mystics such as Bl. Anne Catherine Emmerich and Ven. Mary of Agreda, who documented Mary's life based on revelations, state that Our Lady faced a barrage of diabolic attacks throughout her life. These mystics also relate that the demons were set on destroying her after Jesus' death because of the good she was doing for the Early Church. She was tempted like no other, save

---

[276] Fr. Pius, in discussion with Patrick O'Hearn, September 2024.

[277] Fr. Vincent Lampert, in discussion with Patrick O'Hearn, August 2024.

[278] Ripperger, "Our Lady of Sorrows and Healing."

her Son, by the demons, and the demons unsuccessfully incited her to commit the slightest sin, but she always overcame temptation by having recourse to God, even to the point of weeping.[279]

The demons not only hate Mary, they also fear her. Fr. Alphonsus reported, "Senior exorcists seem to agree that the demons fear her even more so than God, perhaps, because it drives them crazy that she's a mere human being.... It really humbles them, it strikes their pride, that this little woman would have such an authority and power over them."[280] Fr. Benedict agreed, "The devil is actually more afraid of Mary than he is of Jesus.... Because he (the devil) can blaspheme the Lord, and he does. But when he begins to approach Our Lady—he's a goner. The Lord won't stand for it."[281] In one exorcism, a demon even admitted that "Mary is the terror of Hell. She sovereignly loves mortal beings. Her love for mortals is inconceivable. She snatches away more souls than all the angels and all the saints put together."[282] Perhaps this is one of the main reasons why many exorcists have an image of Our Lady, along with a crucifix, present during their exorcisms.

Fr. Amorth related the following story that one of his exorcist friends, Fr. Negrini, told him. When Fr. Negrini asked a demon why it had such a terror of the Virgin Mary, the demon replied, "Because she is the most humble of all and I am the most proud; because she is the most obedient and I am the most rebellious (toward God); and because she is the most pure and I am the

---

[279] Raphael Brown, *The Life of Mary as Seen by the Mystics* (Charlotte, NC: Tan Books, 2012), 52.

[280] Fr. Alphonsus, in discussion with Charles D. Fraune, August 2024.

[281] Fr. Benedict, in discussion with Patrick O'Hearn, December 2024.

[282] Bamonte, *The Virgin Mary and the Devil in Exorcisms*, 43.

vilest."[283] Fr. Amorth described another instance in which his mentor, Fr. Candido, asked the devil: "'Why are you more afraid when I invoke Mary than when I implore God Himself?' He responded: 'I feel more humiliated being conquered by a simple creature than by God Himself.'"[284] Just as without Mary, there can be no Incarnate Jesus, so also without Mary, there can be no victory in the spiritual battle, no true liberation for one who is possessed. Our Lady prays for everyone "afflicted by the devil, and the Lord granted her the power of protecting all who turn to her when they are tempted."[285] Mary is the only creature to never succumb to sin, the only creature who perfectly fulfilled the will of God, the only creature to have always conquered the devil. And so the devil is Mary's slave.

Mary's Role in Exorcism

What is Mary's specific role in exorcisms? Does she just humiliate the devil, or does her presence signal something more? And when is she most powerful? Fr. Lampert provided some keen insights:

> I think she's very powerful. Demons struggled to say her name. Oftentimes, they'll say "that one," "What is *she* doing here?" "Who invited *her* here?" Any exorcist will tell you that if you're dealing with a case and it seems to be stagnated and you're not sure what to do, the invocation of the Blessed Mother will make it happen. One exorcism, where I told the demon to say, "Hail Mary, full of grace," and initially the demon said, "Hail grace of full,"

[283] Amorth and Stanzione, *The Devil Is Afraid of Me*, 97.
[284] Amorth, *An Exorcist Explains the Demonic*, 123.
[285] Brown, *The Life of Mary as Seen by the Mystics*, 242.

scrambling the words and couldn't say the name of Mary. But then, when the demon was finally submitted to the power and the authority of Christ, the demon said, "Hail Mary, full of grace," shrieks and screams: the demon is gone.[286]

Our Lady does not always appear in exorcisms, and she rarely says anything. But when she does show up in an exorcism, it usually means the end is near. Fr. Szada noted, "When the Blessed Mother shows up in a session, the demons can't handle that and they're out of there, so that's usually a sign: this session has come to an end."[287] As the end is approaching, Fr. Szada and his team starts chanting the *Salve Regina*. "That's where the demons really freak; they don't like that at all! That's usually when she shows up, right when we're singing that song. That's the close of the sessions."[288]

Fr. Amorth once said that Mary is "truly the mediatrix of all graces, because she is always the one who obtains the liberation of the demon."[289] Fr. Ripperger also emphasized Mary's role in bringing an exorcism to an end: "As soon as she shows up, it is over."[290] Fr. Ripperger indicated that demons display a specific look of panic when their time is up—similar to someone being pushed off a tall bridge or building—and the demons offer little to no resistance when Mary arrives. Fr. Ripperger compared Our

---

[286] Fr. Vincent Lampert, in discussion with Patrick O'Hearn, August 2024.

[287] Fr. John Szada, in discussion with Patrick O'Hearn, August 2024.

[288] Ibid.

[289] Amorth and Stanzione, *The Devil Is Afraid of Me*, 78.

[290] Fr. Chad Ripperger, "Mary's Role in Spiritual Warfare," March 2, 2022, by Full Sheen Ahead, YouTube, https://www.youtube.com/watch?v=ylHbccuHkTo.

Lady to a nuclear bomb and added that the Blessed Mother shows up in about sixty to seventy percent of his cases.[291] Adam Blai argued that Mary appears less frequently in exorcisms, but he agreed about her role in them: "Mary is always feared, but it's rare that she arrives and the demons or demoniac sees her. If she arrives visually to them, it's usually because the case is about to end entirely."[292] And when Mary does show up in exorcisms, the demons run:

> She has no need to discuss the matter with the demon, or request that they leave; if Our Lady comes to send them off, they run without hesitation. The description that Fr. Ripperger gives is quite startling. He says, "You can tell something's going on [inside the possessed]. Our Lady will appear, they will literally see the abyss open up, they will feel the demon getting ripped out, they will see it going down into the abyss, it closes, and she leaves. She literally doesn't have to say a thing. That's how powerful she is." Father once invoked Our Lady during a possession and the demon started panicking, saying, "Oh no, oh no! Not Her!"[293]

Finally, Fr. Ripperger explained that before major Marian feast days such as the Feast of the Immaculate Conception and the Annunciation, Satanists ramp up their activity by offering Black Masses,[294] and so the possessed often experience greater

---

[291] Ripperger, "Mary's Role in Spiritual Warfare."

[292] Adam Blai, in discussion with Patrick O'Hearn, October 2024.

[293] Fraune, *Slaying Dragons*, 66.

[294] Fr. Chad Ripperger, "Exclusive Interview with Renowned Exorcist Fr. Chad Ripperger." A Black Mass is a ceremony celebrated by Satanic groups that mocks the Catholic Mass. During a Black Mass, Satanists often desecrate a consecrated Host.

suffering at these times. But when the Marian feast day occurs, things calm down. Several exorcists have testified that Our Lady is more powerful in exorcisms on her feast days, specifically on the Solemnities of Mary, such as the Assumption, the Immaculate Conception, and Mary, Mother of God.

Stories of Possession and Our Lady

As with all the saints who show up during exorcisms, the exorcists do not see Our Lady, the demons or the possessed person see her. But when Our Lady does show up, she brings with her an overwhelming sense of peace as proof of her presence. Fr. Pius declared, "I would say also that there's a powerful experience of the presence of the Mother of God as an exorcism is wrapping up. This presence brings a tremendous amount of peace to the room, to the people praying, and even to the demoniac."[295]

Msgr. Rossetti described how he once witnessed Our Lady cast out Satan himself:

> In one case we had in which Lucifer himself was personally present, Mary appeared at the end and cast him out. Whenever she appears, bearing the light of Christ, demons flee. There is no true exorcist or exorcism team that does not rely heavily on Mary. She figures prominently in the Rite of Exorcism, new and old.[296]

He explained that she is so powerful because "Mary is the new Light Bearer. Jesus is the Light. Only she who is immaculate and perfectly humble could contain such divine holiness. Anything

---

[295] Fr. Pius, in discussion with Patrick O'Hearn, September 2024.
[296] Rossetti, *Diary of an American Exorcist*, 121.

stained would find such infinite light unbearable. Thus, it is she … who now casts out Lucifer…. She is our Light Bearer; she is our Morning Star."[297]

Adam Blai recounted a striking story of a possessed person seeing the Blessed Mother during the final session:

> He had partly come to his senses while we were praying and saw a woman in the church he had never seen before. He thought this woman had come to pray like the others—as always, we had a number of women there to pray in support—but then he realized that she was approaching from above, from the direction of an ancient icon of Mary that was in the church. He knew it was Mary, the Mother of Jesus, and she was indescribably beautiful. Mary looked at him and smiled, then turned to Satan and frowned. And all she said was, "It's over," and in a split second, the person felt like a hand reached in and pulled half of him out of himself. He suddenly knew with absolute clarity that it was over.[298]

Fr. Bamonte described a case in which Our Lady even made a demon weep:

> At a certain point the demon said, "There is even that one dressed in white who is telling me that I must go because the time has arrived." The demon said these words with anger and sobbing. Then the demon continued saying,

---

[297] Ibid. In Scripture, Satan is also called "Lucifer," meaning "light bearer." However, his light was extinguished when he rebelled against God, and his power pales in comparison to the humble maiden of Nazareth, whose obedience brought forth the true Light of the World.

[298] Blai, *The Exorcism Files*, 193-194.

"That one is grabbing me. She is grabbing me with that mantle. I cannot take her anymore!" A few minutes passed, and the demon began to shout, "Do not cry. Do not cry. No, nooo, noooo!" Here, we understood that the Virgin Mary was offering her tears to Jesus for the liberation of one of her daughters.[299]

Our Lady of Sorrows is indeed the secret weapon of exorcists. One tear or sigh of Our Lady is more powerful than all of the prayers of saints combined. After all, the demons call her "the thief of souls,"[300] and one of her great titles in the Litany of Loreto is "Comfort of the Afflicted." Our Lady longs to help those most afflicted on the earth, especially those possessed by demons.

Sealing Demonic Portals

In St. Luke's Gospel, Jesus describes the return of the unclean spirit, providing one of the most striking illustrations of exorcism:

> When the unclean spirit has gone out of a man, he passes through waterless places seeking rest; and finding none he says, "I will return to my house from which I came." And when he comes he finds it swept and put in order. Then he goes and brings seven other spirits more evil than himself, and they enter and dwell there; and the last state of that man becomes worse than the first. (Luke 11:24–26)

When a house is not guarded, the enemy can more easily attack. But Our Lady "seals up the portals of entry"[301] according to

---

[299] Bamonte, *The Virgin Mary and the Devil in Exorcisms*, 168.
[300] Amorth, *An Exorcist Explains the Demonic*, 127.
[301] Fr. Pius, in discussion with Patrick O'Hearn, September 2024.

Fr. Pius. He further added, "She goes around and makes sure that they can't come back and can't bring any of their friends, their collaborators, with them. So she's the one who is the closer who 'seals the deal' of deliverance, but she's also the one who prevents any re-admittance."[302] Our Lady keeps the demons locked out; she is the ultimate home and soul security system.

Our Lady is the Queen of Heaven and earth. In medieval literature, she was also sometimes referred to as "Queen of Hell," which, so there is no confusion, solely refers to her absolute power, in union with her Son, over the infernal realm. We find this title in the writings of St. Alphonsus Liguori: "Not only is the most Blessed Virgin Queen of Heaven and of all saints, but she is also Queen of Hell and of all evil spirits."[303] St. Bernard adds, "As a slave conquered in war, [the devil] is forced always to obey the commands of this queen."[304] Although the title "Queen of Hell" is not an official title for Mary in the Church, these saints suggest that Mary has dominion over the demons through her virtue: she is queen by the conquest of her Son.[305] She is also the Gate of Heaven and not only slams the door on Satan's proud face but also keeps it permanently closed. And so if we want to stay protected from diabolical attacks, even possession, we must stay devoted to the Blessed Mother.

One of the most powerful ways for us to shield ourselves from diabolical influence and to keep ourselves under Our Lady's mantle is by praying the Rosary.[306] As the saying goes, praying a

---

302 Fr. Pius, in discussion with Patrick O'Hearn, September 2024.

303 St. Alphonsus Liguori, *The Glories of Mary* (Charlotte, NC: TAN Books, 2012), 115.

304 Ibid., 118.

305 See Fraune, *Slaying Dragons*, 148.

306 Fr. Benedict asked his prayer team (consisting of twenty-five people) to pray four Rosaries and the Chaplet of St. Michael the

Rosary each day keeps the devil at bay. The Rosary is a whip that beats the hell out of the devil. Or as one demon told Fr. Bamonte, "You are hurting me with those little beads, bastards!"[307] The foul-mouthed demons are tortured by those who love Our Lady and pray her Rosary, and they beg the exorcists to put the Rosary away.

On one occasion, Fr. Benedict was praying the Rosary during an exorcism. At the time, he was a young priest and was offering prayer support to another priest. When he started praying the Rosary, "all Hell broke loose. But Our Lady kept it contained.[308] Real progress was finally made, despite him not performing an exorcism. It is for this reason that Fr. Benedict could say that "devotion to the Blessed Virgin Mary … is the greatest key to deliverance and to exorcism."[309] And so Mary continues to crush the ancient dragon.

Archangel before and during his exorcisms. As a result, he would see immediate deliverance: "We always had victories," he said.

[307] Bamonte, *The Virgin Mary and the Devil in Exorcisms*, 109.

[308] Fr. Benedict, in discussion with Patrick O'Hearn, December 2024.

[309] Ibid.

8

A Renewed Devotion
to the Saints

The power of the saints in exorcisms shows us that the saints possess a role and an authority in the Kingdom of Heaven that must not be overlooked. They shine upon us the light that they themselves merited, through Christ, by the holiness of their lives on earth. They call to us by their writings, through the history of their lives, and now from their heavenly thrones. From there, through the bond of grace and the unity established by the Holy Spirit, they are evermore our brothers and sisters, wise and good and capable of coming to our aid.

The saints, therefore, should be treated like members of our family, like the best of friends. They are at the same time the most noble of advocates, the most powerful of princes, the mightiest of soldiers, the wisest of the wise, and the most generous of benefactors. We should look upon them not as distant relations or as pleasant memories from the past: they are with us here and now, and we must nurture a deep love for them and a true friendship with them.

The fruits of this friendship reflect the specific ways in which they can come to our aid: they show us and help us become who we are meant to be, they assist us in imitating them and acquiring their same virtues, they encourage and enable us to persevere until the end, they share the gifts and the graces they have received, and they help us to stay focused on Christ and to fear nothing but sin. The saints say to us, with St. Paul, "Be imitators of me, as I am of Christ" (1 Cor. 11:1).

The saints imitated Christ, and so all that they do is "always pointing to Christ," Fr. Lampert said. "They're never pointing to themselves. Their wills are united with the will of God. . . . I think the saints, in one sense, are also bringing a message from God. They never want the focus to be on themselves; they always want the focus to be on God."[310] And the way in which they followed Christ, which they now hold out to us that we may do likewise, is through their virtues. Fr. Lampert added,

> I think the key is, with any saint, what virtue do they exemplify? And then learning that virtue: how do we mimic that in our own lives? If we can look to some virtue that the saints really exemplify, we can apply it to our lives. It helps us to join the Communion of Saints in Heaven.[311]

Fr. Timothy likewise spoke of the virtues of the saints, recounting a pilgrimage he took with a mystic:

> I traveled to Europe to visit the tombs of some of the great saints with one of the spiritual sensitives who assists us in our ministry.[312] Her connection with the saints was such

---

[310] Fr. Vincent Lampert, in discussion with Patrick O'Hearn, August 2024.

[311] Ibid.

[312] Fr. Timothy is here referring to a Catholic layman with an approved spiritual gift who assists exorcists in their ministry. See

that we were able to record dictations of what numerous saints (like Padre Pio, Augustine, and Maria Goretti) would communicate to her. They spoke with a gentle clarity and encouraged us to imitate them in their heroic virtues. It brings a very exciting sense that the saints are truly very close by![313]

The acquisition of these virtues is dependent upon the gradual conformity of the mind, heart, and will of a person to the will of God through prayer, fasting, and works of charity. Penance, as a general term to include many different practices, is essential here. Our fallen human nature leads us to become attached to this present and passing world and to created things that often become like gods in our lives and frustrate our efforts to maintain an undivided loyalty to Our Lord Jesus Christ. But penance allows us to break free of these attachments and focus on the world to come, which is our true home. After all, the saints are the teachers and examples upon which we may pattern our spiritual lives, and one thing they proclaim, like the Angel at Fatima, is "Penance!"

Fr. Szada discussed the importance of the saints as models for penance. He said, "We have got to recover Catholic practice and Catholic identity, among which is the ascetical practices of the Church: fasting in particular." Commenting on the saints' willingness to suffer for the sake of the Kingdom, he added,

Look at the lives of our saints: the ascetical practices, keeping vigil in the Church, sometimes all night long. All of

---

Charles D. Fraune, *The Occult Among Us: Exorcists and Former Occultists Expose the Nature of This Modern Evil* (Charlotte, NC: Slaying Dragons Press, 2024), chap. 22, on spiritually gifted Catholics who work with exorcists.

[313] Fr. Timothy, in discussion with Charles D. Fraune, August 2024.

those kinds of things are very, very important: fasting and abstinence.... There's where I think we can learn from the saints: the kind of ascetical practices that they practiced that were very important. We don't know how to embrace the cross anymore. We don't know how to willingly suffer. I think our saints can teach us that.[314]

To take up the Christian life requires a resolve to let the "old man" pass away and the "new man" (in Christ) grow to maturity (see 2 Cor. 5:17). We must invite God in and let God operate in all aspects of our lives, and we cannot do this without penance.

However, inviting God into our lives, Fr. Lampert said, is even more difficult than casting out a demon; but once again, we can turn to the saints as our perfect aids. He explained,

I tell people that in an exorcism, casting the devil out is actually the easy part. The harder part is getting the person to invite God in, and I think that's what the saints do: they teach us the importance of inviting God into our lives. Oftentimes, people that are dealing with the demonic know they're in a moment of crisis, and so they recognize that they need God. But once that crisis is passed, sometimes they forget about that. But the saints, I think, tell us to give God His rightful place in our lives. So the saints are not only powerful in helping to get the demons to leave, they're also powerful in helping us to invite God to enter.[315]

Once we "let God in," we must persevere in this resolution and hold fast to the Faith. This perseverance is a gift from God that

---

[314] Fr. John Szada, in discussion with Patrick O'Hearn, August 2024.

[315] Fr. Vincent Lampert, in discussion with Patrick O'Hearn, August 2024.

the saints teach we must daily ask God to sustain. One of the best ways to persevere untiringly is to maintain our trust in the goodness and mercy of God. In the light of the constant failures that Christians face in their spiritual journey, Fr. Lampert counseled:

> I think one of the things the saints want us to know is that we don't have to be perfect. One of the names for Satan is *the accuser*; he gets us to give in to sin, trying to objectify evil, presenting evil as something good, and then, once we do, the devil is there to accuse us, like, "Look at you, look at what you've done," trying to make us feel bad and give in to a sense of guilt. But I think the saints want us to know that the greatest things we could know in life are not the sins we commit but God's love and mercy: that's greater than any sin that we can commit, if we're willing to accept it.[316]

The saints not only counsel, advise, and inspire, they also intercede. It is this intercession that, even more than the witness they left behind in their earthly lives, imparts to us a most powerful aid. The merits that they have won as a result of the good deeds they did as members of the Mystical Body of Christ are spiritual goods that they can share with us on earth.[317] When

---

[316] Ibid.

[317] This idea is known as the "treasury of merits," also called the "treasury of satisfactions" or the "treasury of the Church." It is the spiritual treasury containing the infinite merits of Christ, "the immense [and] unfathomable" merits of Our Lady, and those of all the saints. These merits are the result of Christ's perfect work of our Redemption and the cooperation that Our Lady and the saints contribute, to varying degrees, by their holy lives. See CCC 1471–1478.

asked whether it would be proper to ask the saints for a share in their spiritual gifts and virtues, just as Elisha did of Elijah before he was assumed into Heaven (see 2 Kings 2:9), Fr. Pius replied,

> Yes, and I think that's a great instinct there. I think that the Church lifts up these saints, these holy ones, for our veneration and for our interest precisely for this reason. They show us some aspect of the Christian life which we are meant to imitate, or at least strive after, some particular path or virtue: the humility of Our Lady, the penitence of St. Mary Magdalene, the quiet devotion to duty of St. Joseph, and so forth.[318]

The saints are truly our role models, our older brethren, the veterans of our common spiritual war, whose triumph has not simply merited for them a crown and eternal rest but the ability to bestow upon us their own strength, simultaneously calling us and lifting us to the glory they have received.

On a Saint's Feast Day

Fr. Pius answered the question of whether the saints had a greater power and grace to assist us on their feast days with a strong "Yes." Explaining further, he highlighted the fact that the saints in Heaven are glorified:

> There's an expression about when a saint is canonized, that they are lifted up, exalted, specifically, they are "raised to the altar." They are given the privilege of being glorified at the altars of Christendom in the Holy Sacrifice of the

---

[318] Fr. Pius, in discussion with Patrick O'Hearn, September 2024.

Mass. They're honored by that, they're commemorated with the Holy Sacrifice of the Mass. So their feast days are days when they are especially glorified by the Church. It is on these days that the saints, speaking figuratively, shine with a greater luster, as the Church is honoring them and praying to them.[319]

As an example of this "greater luster," we can look at the Church's tradition of blessing certain sacramentals that coincide with the life or work of a particular saint, such as blessed palms on the feast of St. Peter Verona or blessed wine on the feast of St. Blase. These blessings are specifically performed on the feast day of the saint. While they can be done on other days as an exception, these blessings are fixed on these days due to the Church's belief that the saints exert a more focused intercession on the day the Church honors them.

Further, on some of the greater feast days of the Church, in the ordinary form of the Roman rite, the priest bestows a blessing that makes evident the connection between that feast and the availability of special graces unique to the day. For example, the Solemn Blessing for the Mass on the Feast of the Immaculate Conception states, "May you, who have devoutly gathered on this day, carry away with you the gifts of spiritual joys and heavenly rewards." It is *on this day* that these "gifts of spiritual joys and heavenly rewards" are afforded to those who joined the Church in devoutly honoring the feast.

On a saint's feast day, there is also another significant reality present. Fr. Pius explained,

The efficacy on those feast days is more about the fact that you have all of the Church remembering the saint and

---

[319] Ibid.

being devoted to them, so there's an increased devotion throughout all of Holy Church on those days. That helps to make their intercessory power all the more efficacious. Our prayer, especially our liturgical prayer, is something that God accounts for in His dispensation of grace throughout the Church.[320] So we have something to do with that: the devotion that we bring to the table on, for example, the Feast of the Immaculate Conception, means that our intercessory power through that mystery is going to be all the greater that day.[321]

The great saints themselves have, in their earthly lives, experienced this same special intercession of a saint on that saint's feast day. The biography of St. Alphonsus Liguori, for example, whose life is a tremendous witness of countless aspects of the Christian life, describes how his great patroness, St. Teresa of Ávila, once clearly interceded for him on her feast day, as he credited her intercession for his important discovery of a plot intended to divide his religious congregation, "for it happened between the first and second Vespers of her feast."[322]

Exorcists have also noted this power of intercession on the feast of a saint and will often choose which saints to invoke based on the Church's calendar. Fr. Szada said, "It usually depends on the calendar, for example, what the feast day is. A lot of times, we'll go with a particular saint depending on that particular feast

---

[320] As Pope Pius XII teaches in his encyclical *Mystici Corporis Christi*, "The salvation of many depends on the prayers and voluntary penances which the members of the Mystical Body of Jesus Christ offer" (no. 44).

[321] Fr. Pius, in discussion with Patrick O'Hearn, September 2024.

[322] *The Life of St. Alphonsus Liguori*, 175.

day."[323] Fr. Timothy said that he also invokes the saint whose feast day falls on the day of the exorcism. He said, "On one occasion, I invoked the saint for the day and had horrific reactions from the demon when I did so."[324]

The reality behind these experiences of modern exorcists is reflected in the teachings of the great sixteenth-century exorcist Fr. Menghi, who, in his book, *The Scourge of Demons*, said:

> Again, it is often found that exorcisms are more powerful and efficacious on days of greater holiness and sacred solemnity, such as the Solemnities of the Nativity, Resurrection, and Ascension of Our Lord, the feast of Pentecost, and other such days. Also exorcisms tend to be more effective and efficacious on feasts, or the vigils of the feasts, of the Blessed Virgin Mary, the apostles, and other significant holy festivities.[325]

St. Paul compared the glory of the saints with the varying glories of the heavens, stating, "There is one glory of the sun, and another glory of the moon, and another glory of the stars; for star differs from star in glory. So is it with the resurrection of the dead" (1 Cor 15:41–42). As each star is given its fixed place in the sky, and as certain heavenly bodies often shine more brightly at one time of the year more than the others do, so each saint shines with a special supernatural luster on his or her fixed day in the liturgical calendar.

---

[323] Fr. John Szada, in discussion with Patrick O'Hearn, August 2024.
[324] Fr. Timothy, in discussion with Charles D. Fraune, August 2024.
[325] Menghi, *The Scourge of Demons*, 72.

The Role of Our Patron Saints

Fr. Timothy said that he very frequently invokes the patron saints of the possessed person during an exorcism session.[326] This is also something that Fr. Szada always does.[327] Fr. Lampert agreed, saying, "Absolutely."[328] Fr. Alphonsus said that he does this sometimes too, adding, "But, as with other things, you don't always see the same reaction."[329] Fr. Athanasius said, "If you invoke the patron saint of the energumen, that can often create unpleasantness for the demon."[330]

Fr. Pius explained how someone's patron saint will intercede for that person:

In our Baptism, we're given a name, and that name has this connection with the saint whose name we bear. As a result, there's a real relationship there, of patronage, which is a powerful and real relationship. The saints in Heaven claim us as their own if we bear their name, and our parents or godparents have set that up in an authoritative way at the baptismal font, this relationship of patronage. The Confirmation name is also a powerful one because the person has chosen it themselves, in some way, usually; so there's some complicity on the part of the one being confirmed.

[326] Fr. Timothy, in discussion with Charles D. Fraune, August 2024.

[327] Fr. John Szada, in discussion with Patrick O'Hearn, August 2024. However, he added that he does not ("don't usually do that") invoke the saint who bears the same name as the possessed.

[328] Fr. Vincent Lampert, in discussion with Patrick O'Hearn, August 2024. This was specifically about the patron of the name of the possessed.

[329] Fr. Alphonsus, in discussion with Charles D. Fraune, August 2024.

[330] Fr. Athanasius, in discussion with Charles D. Fraune, October 2024.

So those relationships of patronage are real; they're not just imaginary. The saints want us to lean into those relationships of patronage probably more than we do; they're taking that relationship seriously and they're hoping that we will too. The demons recognize that; they're legalists. They understand that patronage and they understand that if I were to invoke St. Barbara in praying for someone who bears the name "Barbara," the demons would have to respect that, even though they hate it. It really is a powerful defense against demonic influence in our life.[331]

Indeed, the Church teaches that "a name expresses a person's essence and identity and the meaning of this person's life" (CCC 203), and so parents are often motivated to assign sacred names of the saints to their children. Their child then continuously hears this holy name whenever he is addressed, and the ever-attentive patron in Heaven keeps his gaze upon the child with a particular spiritual affection.

The Saints Choose Us

When it comes to someone's personal devotional life, Fr. Pius said,

The saints choose us more than we choose them. I have seen this to be true and have seen it many times in my priestly life. I think that if we can help people understand that if they find a particular attraction or devotion in their heart to some particular saint, or story of a saint, or style of spiritual writing, or something like that, that it's good for

---

[331] Fr. Pius, in discussion with Patrick O'Hearn, September 2024.

us to lean into that and trust that those saints are wanting to be involved in our spiritual lives.[332]

Fr. Timothy highly encouraged Catholics to pay attention to the small ways that the saints are trying to get our attention. He said,

> The saints really, with such great laughter, encircle us and laugh and they say, "If only you would call on us! We love you very much, but you never call on us! We think of you like sleepwalkers, because you don't even seem to show an awareness that we're around and the Lord wants us to help you. Ask now!"

Fr. Timothy also discussed a certain mystic, approved by her bishop, who wrote about St. Philomena appearing to her. According to this mystic, St. Philomena would likewise say, "You are like sleepwalkers. We [the saints] drop things in front of you, like a holy card or something—do not disregard that! That's how we try to communicate with you. Wake up and realize that we're here for you."[333]

This ignorance of the attempts of the saints to get our attention was also mentioned by Fr. Pius, who said, "Sometimes we can mistrust or fail to listen to those nudgings of inspiration that, I think, come through the intercessory power of the saints." And if a person has a particular devotion to a saint, he advised that that person should take up the prayers and writings the saint has left behind. He explained,

---

[332] Ibid.

[333] Fr. Timothy, in discussion with Charles D. Fraune, August 2024. Here, Father refers to the mysterious reason behind why we may, one day, find or be given a specific holy card.

Some might have a particular devotion to, for example, St. Patrick: they love St. Patrick, they love his story through his biography. Well, then, they should pray the Breastplate of St. Patrick, because there's a connection there that St. Patrick wants to have with that soul, and that prayer is part of his patrimony to the Church."[334]

Fr. Athanasius once relayed a fascinating insight resulting from his encounter with a demon during an exorcism. In one exorcism, the demon told Fr. Athanasius, "There's a black priest who has had your back for five years." Later, he had to think about who that might be, if the demon was in fact telling the truth, which he suspected to be the case. In his research, when considering the other details the demon mentioned about that priest, he found an article he had once read about Augustus Tolton that discussed the beginning of the process of his canonization.[335] Fr. Athanasius said, "I then remembered that I had said a prayer at that time for his cause for canonization. I remembered the prayer, that I had said the prayer, and that I did so and forgot, simply moved on. Venerable Augustus must have been grateful for that prayer for his cause and stuck with me."[336]

We asked Fr. Timothy, from his experience, if he thinks that the saints reciprocate when we demonstrate affection for them or nurture a devotion to them. He said, "Absolutely." He explained, saying, "Do I think that St. Mary Magdalene de Pazzi paid greater

---

[334] Fr. Pius, in discussion with Patrick O'Hearn, September 2024.

[335] Ven. Augustus Tolton died in 1897; his cause was opened by Cardinal Francis George of Chicago in 2010, and he was declared venerable by Pope Francis in June 2019.

[336] Fr. Athanasius, in discussion with Charles D. Fraune, July 2024.

attention to me, or showed an affinity toward me, after I visited her tomb? Absolutely, without a moment's hesitation."[337]

Fr. Athanasius likewise said that he has noticed an increase in the assistance of St. Joseph the more he has entrusted himself to him: "I have noticed that, after my consecration to St. Joseph, St. Joseph is more active in my cases. This shows that we have to do our part as well."[338]

While the saints take an active interest in our spiritual welfare, they, like Our Lord, need us to respond to their invitations and show that we truly desire their help and are willing to work alongside them. When we make the decision to respond to the invitations of Our Lord and His saints, we allow Heaven's assistance to more readily come to us. It is then that the floodgates of grace are allowed to open.

Devotions to the Saints

The Catholic Faith is infinitely rich and powerful in its supernatural wealth and strength. Concretely, the number of the sanctified in Heaven who are ready and waiting for us to call upon them is staggering. Given the great number of devotions that the Church recommends to the faithful, it is therefore helpful to have some recommendations as to which saints to call upon so the average Catholic will know how best to make use of these tremendous spiritual allies.

An important perspective that Fr. Pius always counsels people to have is that "there are seasons in the spiritual life." In other words, our devotions will often change throughout our lives, and

---

[337] Fr. Timothy, in discussion with Charles D. Fraune, August 2024.
[338] Fr. Athanasius, in discussion with Charles D. Fraune, July 2024.

there is no reason for us to prevent or be worried about this shift. Fr. Pius continued:

> That's an expression I use very often with people who come to me for spiritual direction. We have to not feel compelled to pile up devotions in our spiritual lives, hanging on to each devotion that, at some point, was very significant in my life. It might be that you're a great friend of St. Thérèse for a while, and then you get married and you enter a different season in your life [and] you have somebody else who's close to you. Just like in our personal relationships, so too with the saints: it might be that you love St. Thérèse and then now you love her parents because they have a greater voice in your life. St. Thérèse is not offended, believe me! We mustn't be compelled by guilt or fear to do things in our spiritual lives.[339]

In fact, the saints will very often point us to other saints and, essentially, hand us off to them. Fr. Pius compared this action of the saints to an event in his own life: When he was younger, he went on a visit to a certain religious order, but while he was there, he was pointed in the direction of a different religious order. He explained,

> This friend of mine, who was an Oratorian, said St. Philip Neri, while he was alive, used to do that all the time: he used to suggest to young people to join this or that religious Order, but not necessarily to become a member of his own congregation: he pointed the way. The saints still do that. St. Thérèse might point you to her parents. St.

---

[339] Fr. Pius, in discussion with Patrick O'Hearn, September 2024.

Joseph might point you to St. Joseph of Cupertino. St. Francis might point somebody to St. Padre Pio. So these seasons of devotion are absolutely part and parcel of the Catholic devotional life; we have to follow those inclinations and not feel guilty or afraid that somehow we're doing something wrong by not living our spiritual lives like we did when we were twelve![340]

When we feel drawn to a certain saint, or when we sense that a certain saint is trying to get our attention, there are some practical things we can do to nurture this friendship. First, if possible, we should attend Mass in honor of that saint on his or her feast day. On other days, we can add our saint's name to the end of the Rosary, invoke our saint when making an act of thanksgiving after Holy Communion, or call upon our saint frequently throughout the day. Fr. Pius also recommended the practice of making a holy hour of prayer *with our saint*, inviting him or her to be our companion during that time spent with Our Lord.

No matter which saint you form a personal devotion to, one practical way to welcome all the saints' help into your spiritual life is simply by following the liturgical calendar. Fr. Pius agreed, stating, "Let the liturgy of the Church guide us. We are liturgical creatures as Catholics. The Church year and her calendar are what's meant to guide our devotional life."[341]

Concretely, what does it look like to let the Church calendar guide our spiritual lives? Fr. Pius provided a specific example:

If you don't feel like you have a particular devotion to St. Joseph, for example, well, when Wednesday rolls around,

[340] Ibid.
[341] Ibid.

you might just remember, well, Wednesday traditionally is the day that we think of St. Joseph, every week, so maybe that would be a good day to say the Litany of St. Joseph, even if you don't have a particular devotion to him.[342]

We should also remember that on a saint's feast day, the Mass and its specific prayers and the Liturgy of the Hours are all in the saint's honor. The Church has that saint on her mind throughout the day, and as was mentioned, the saints have a greater efficacy and intercessory power on their feast days. As Fr. Pius added, "So there's a reason for us to at least think of them that day, even if we're not particularly devoted to them."[343]

Within the Communion of Saints is an intense exchange of spiritual goods, and by the gift and grace of Baptism, we are participators in this great exchange. Indeed, communion with Our Lord is not just something we presently long for, to receive only after death; through the Holy Eucharist and the other channels of supernatural grace, we experience now a foretaste of the joys and strengths we will realize in full in Heaven. It is the same with the saints: we do not have to wait until eternity to enjoy the company of the citizens of Heaven. They are given to us here, now, and they desire to be our companions on the way.

[342] Ibid.
[343] Ibid.

Conclusion

The glorious work of the Redemption of Our Lord Jesus Christ has incorporated Christians into the Kingdom of Heaven and has given us a Divine King, an immaculate Queen, mighty princes, and countless royal citizens whose glory is a mirror of the Son of God, our Savior. Thus, in a time when man feels as though he is alone and in his darkest hour, we must become acutely aware that these royal citizens of glory, the saints, are present with us, powerful, and yearning to intercede for us.

Our struggle with sin, in which we fight to maintain our communion with Christ and our salvation, threatens to draw us into the darkness of depression, fear, despair, division, addiction, family strife, loss of friendships, loss of faith, loss of love for Our Lord, and—when we feel over-burdened by this long struggle—into a compromise with evil as we lay down our arms and quit the battle. But it is in these moments of absolute darkness, when our wills are nearly overcome by evil, that the saints desire the most to help us. Like God, who loves to forgive us and loves to save us from the snares of Satan, the saints love to be given a chance to help us.

A Capuchin priest once related that he had received a statue of St. Padre Pio, but since he was not particularly fond of it, as it was not very beautiful, he placed it on his bookshelf, somewhat out of sight. One day, he heard an interior voice say, "Why don't you honor me?" St. Padre Pio was rebuking the priest for his lack of devotion. At that moment, the priest had also felt that St. Padre Pio clearly wanted to help him, if he would only seek his intercession. And so the priest began to ask St. Padre Pio for his prayers, and he regularly felt the presence of this great patron afterward and throughout his life.

The power of the protection and intercession that the saints can give depends greatly on how much we invoke their aid. In order to comprehend the saints' desire to help us, we should bear in mind Our Lady's apparition to St. Catherine of Labouré in 1830, in which Our Lady held a small, golden globe topped with a cross, and rays of light emanated from her fingers, which were adorned with many jewels and precious stones. Our Lady told St. Catherine, "The ball which you see represents the whole world, especially France, and each person in particular. These rays symbolize the graces I shed upon those who ask for them. The gems from which rays do not fall are the graces for which souls forget to ask."[344]

The eagerness of the saints to assist us is much greater than our willingness to call upon them. They desire for us to receive all the graces necessary for our salvation. Yet we can easily push the saints out of our minds, and, as we see in the apparition of Our Lady, when we forget about the saints, their heavenly resources cannot be obtained. The saints love nothing other than Jesus and making Jesus known, and their resources are aids to our communion with Jesus. And so when our love for the saints wanes, so often does our love for Jesus.

---

[344] Joseph I. Dirvin, C.M., *Saint Catherine Labouré of the Miraculous Medal* (New York: Farrar, Straus and Cudahy Inc., 1958), 93.

It remains a mystery why some saints appear in exorcisms while others do not, but one thing is certain: the saints are active in Heaven, and even more so than they were on earth. A demon once spoke through a possessed woman to St. John Vianney: "How thou makest me suffer! If there were three men on earth like thyself, my kingdom would be destroyed."[345] If this power was present in a saint still "running the race," imagine the power he would wield after he victoriously crossed the finished line! Now he and all the saints long to share this power with us. For those living in mortal sin and on the path to Hell, the saints urge us to change our ways. For those striving for sanctity, the saints encourage us to persevere. For those who suffer beneath the devil's power, the saints desire our complete liberation. After all, the saints want nothing more than for us to join them forever in Heaven, to gaze upon the greatest sight for all eternity: the Beatific Vision. For the saints are our best friends and greatest allies, especially in our darkest moments when it seems as though the gates of Hell are prevailing against us. It is precisely in these dark moments that we need to turn to the intercession of the saints so we may more effectively obtain God's favor and blessing.

The saints' power to intercede communicates to us the truth that we are not alone. These glorious citizens of the Kingdom of Heaven, who overflow with the love of God and of souls, are willing to share every grace, every strength, every virtue, and every merit that they earned through many struggles, many risings, and many glorious victories over sin and evil. Moreover, their constant victories in the face of evil remind us, as Fr. Pius said, that "we're already victorious, we're already saved, we're already washed in

---

[345] Fr. Bartholomew O'Brien, *The Curé of Ars: Patron Saint of Parish Priests* (Charlotte, NC: TAN Books, 2012), 80.

the Precious Blood of Christ; we already share in His victory, so we don't have anything to be afraid of, really."[346] The saints have become the nemeses of demons and are rightly bewailed by them as their "assassins."

The saints' desire to assist in exorcisms shows that they are willing to get involved in the darkest and vilest parts of our lives, a place where most any other friend would flee in fear. Therefore, we should never feel alone. Because, indeed, we are not alone.

The saints are there for us, like the best of friends—we cannot ignore them!

All you holy saints of God, pray for us!

---

[346] Fr. Pius, in discussion with Patrick O'Hearn, September 2024.

Appendix A

Q & A with the Exorcists

Most of the additional material below was not included explicitly in the previous chapters, though some information is repeated for emphasis. The Q & A is divided into the following sections: The Demons React to the Saints, The Impact of the Saints on the Demons, The Role of Mary, Experiences of the Exorcists, Practices of the Exorcists, Cautions about Curiosity and Revelations, Learning from the Saints, Certain Saints to Invoke, and Devotions for the Faithful.[347]

---

[347] Sources for these interviews are as follows (listed alphabetically): Fr. Alphonsus, in discussion with Charles D. Fraune, August 2024; Fr. Athanasius, in discussion with Charles D. Fraune, July 2024; Fr. Benedict, in discussion with Patrick O'Hearn, December 2024; Fr. Vincent Lampert, in discussion with Patrick O'Hearn, August 2024; Fr. Pius, in discussion with Patrick O'Hearn, September 2024; Fr. John Szada, in discussion with Patrick O'Hearn, August 2024; Fr. Timothy, in discussion with Charles D. Fraune, August 2024.

The Demons React to the Saints

What do the demons say when they see that a saint is present?

Fr. Lampert: I've had exorcisms where there's a reference, "Why is that one here?" And it's a quick reference to St. John Paul II. Sometimes they do name the saint indirectly, like, "That one!" like when it comes to the Blessed Mother. Demons are kind of reluctant to name the saints, but they will say "that one" as a reference, and then you can get them, finally command them, in the Name of Jesus, to say who they see.

Fr. Alphonsus: You will hear the demons say, "Get that one away from me." The priest, using his authority, will ask, "Who are you seeing?" The demon will often make the reference to the saint's presence, saying, "Get that one away from me," or "You stay away," and then the exorcist will use his authority, saying "In the Name of Jesus, who are you seeing?" That's always the way in which the Lord is letting us know, "Hey, this is a saint to really appeal to, to get rid of this demon."

Would the demons have any special way of referring to the saints, since they don't like to use their names?

Fr. Pius: The demons would call Pope St. John Paul II "the white clad one" or "the one dressed in white," referring to his white papal habit or cassock. As I recall, they would say something like referring to St. Gemma Galgani as "the one dressed in black." I think, as a Passionist, she wore a kind of black frock. I also remember one of them calling St. Norbert, a famous exorcist, "that white clad dog," or something like that. And, for Padre Pio, "the bearded one."

How do demons react when a saint becomes present during an exorcism?

Fr. Lampert: They're terrified. They realize that they're in the presence of one who is greater than themselves. So it's fear, and during those times, they're not going to be derogatory. That's probably when they're going to reveal things more of the truth. Demons know the truth, they just reject it. The devil's not an atheist; he knows that God exists, he just wants us to believe that God does not exist and to live in that manner. Even in the Garden of Eden, the serpent said to Eve, "Did God really tell you …?" So he acknowledges the existence of God, and I think when these saints show up, the demons are more compelled to tell the truth. Because demons are liars. The devil is a liar. The father of all lies. You have to be careful that they're not leading you into deception. But when the saints show up, demons are less likely to be able to lie because they're now in the presence of one who truly lived in the light and the truth of God.

The Impact of the Saints on the Demons

Could you explain part of the reason why the demons are so affected by the saints?

Fr. Lampert: I think the reason that demons hate humanity goes back to the Incarnation. Lucifer, before the Fall, wanted God to unite His nature with the angelic nature, but God chose to unite His nature with humans. As a result, Satan hates humans, especially the saints, because he got Adam and Eve, our first parents, to succumb to his temptation, and, in that sense, he felt like he defeated human flesh. But then the saints are those who overcome human weakness and human frailty, and Satan isn't able to attack them. I think that's what infuriates him, that he wants humanity to remain in the darkness, but you have these holy men and women who have stepped out into the light of Christ and are leading others into the light as well. The saints are those who have united their free will with the will of God. That's the battle that takes place: Satan would want us to unite our free will with his rejection of God.

Could you talk about the general idea of why God raises up great saints at certain times in Church history, and how that applies to our own day?

Fr. Lampert: I would begin by saying one of my favorite verses in the Bible is in the Book of Genesis. God says, "Let there be light," and when you think of the saints in general, what's one of the images that we have? The halo around their head. They're not radiating their glory; they're radiating the glory of God. They're kind of a light that shines in the darkness, and they appear at different moments throughout our history. I was reading a book recently and it had comments about the Servant of God Archbishop Fulton Sheen, and he was talking about how we live in a certain period within Christianity, and something different happens every five hundred years or so. You think, in the first five hundred years, it was the fall of the Roman Empire; in the second five hundred years, it was the Great Schism, in 1054; and then five hundred years later, 1517, it's the Protestant Reformation; and now we're living in that next window. The first period, we could say, was due to attacks on the Church's doctrinal teachings; the second period was due to attacks on the head of the Church; the third period was due to attacks on the Church herself; and now the era in which we live, it's the attack on the Person of Christ, really asking if Christ is even relevant anymore. It does seem, though, that whenever darkness tried to overcome the life of the Church, God would call forth holy men and women, the saints, that will become a shining light in that period of darkness.

When you think of the first fall, among the great saints that would come to mind, one of them would obviously be St. Augustine, who would be that light, that saint, that would shine. When you think of the second fall, with the Great Schism, the great saints would include St. Francis and St. Clare. During the third fall, in the time of the Protestant Reformation, the great saints would include St. Ignatius of Loyola. Now, in today's world, who are those saints that God has called forth in a world that's rejecting Christ? You might think of folks like St. Maximilian Kolbe, St. John Paul II, Mother Teresa, and, even recently, the new St. Carlo Acutis. So God always calls forth holy men and women, these saints, to be a light that will shine in the darkness that we experience at different periods within Christian history.

How is it that the modern saints appear more frequently in your work as an exorcist?

Fr. Lampert: I think modern day saints, holy men and women who have shined in the period in which we live, are very powerful. When you look at each of those five-hundred-year periods of Christianity, you can find great saints in any of those eras, but I think the era in which we live—if we truly believe what people say, that we no longer live in Christendom times, that we live in apostolic times, that society and culture today will not allow Christianity to shape its economics, politics, education, nothing; where at one time Christianity was molding and shaping society, now society is rejecting that—we're back to the period of apostolic times where Christianity has to confront a culture that basically knows nothing of Christ or has rejected Christ.

Then you have these holy men and women, these saints of the twentieth and twenty-first centuries who go against that, and the devil would hate that, he would hate that there's shining examples of commitment to Christ in the world today. So the devil wants the light to go out, but these holy men and women, St. Padre Pio and all the other ones that we've mentioned, they keep turning the light on. I think these modern-day saints really speak to us. Young people need a young saint like Carlo Acutis to know that being a faithful person isn't just for certain people of one generation. Here's a young person from their own generation that makes faith relevant, that makes Christ relevant.

The Role of Mary

Why is Mary so great?

Fr. Benedict: She is the Mother of all the saints. The Church teaches that she has more sanctity than all of the saints put together. She is also called the Queen and Mother of Martyrs because she suffered more than all of the martyrs put together. We don't understand the greatness of Our Lady. I'm sorry we have lost our understanding of how great our Mother is. She is the Queen of Heaven and earth forever. She's God's finest creation. She is more powerful than an army decked in battle array. Call on her. Trust her. Pray to her. Ask her to pray. Because God has entrusted victory to her. She is also the Queen of Grace. She's the Queen of Clergy, so she is the Queen of Exorcists as well. And her Son has entrusted her with this gift to crush the head of Satan in an individual, in a family, in a nation, and in the world.

What happens in the exorcism once Our Lady has clearly begun to intercede?

Fr. Lampert: When Mary shows up, the demons know that it's the end game, so to speak, because ultimately, during an exorcism, God is going to determine the day and the timing for the expulsion, and whenever Mary shows up, I know that this is it: this is the moment, this is the day, this is the time, that it's going to end.

Does she always show up?

Fr. Alphonsus: No. In my experience, and in the experience of my exorcist friends, it is not the case that she always shows up.

How often does Our Lady show up in an exorcism?

Fr. Athanasius: In the big cases, Our Lady will show up at the end. She shows up to do the last humiliation, the *coup de gras*. This, however, does not happen in every case.

How is it that Mary appears to be more threatening to the demons than God Himself does?

Fr. Lampert: Here's somebody that said "yes" to God, reversing the "no" of the devil. The devil's going to expect Jesus to do what He does because Jesus is God. Now, with Mary, you're having a human creature, and I think that's something that the demons just cannot accept, that somehow a human creature is defeating them.

Do the demons hate specific titles of Mary?

Fr. Lampert: Yes, because those names and titles speak of her glory and the glory that the demons would want for themselves. But they know that they've lost them forever through their expulsion out of Heaven. The demons are very jealous when they hear titles being given to the saints or to our Blessed Mother. They are titles that they wish would be bestowed upon themselves.

Are there any titles of Mary that seem to be more powerful in exorcisms? And why these?

Fr. Pius: Well, her name, obviously, is a powerful invocation. Beyond that, invoking especially the mystery of her Immaculate Conception and also of Our Lord's Incarnation. So anything having to do with the Incarnation of Our Lord in her womb, the Annunciation of Gabriel—that's why I think the actual prayer, the Hail Mary, is such a powerful prayer in exorcism, and also reading those passages from the Gospel of St. Luke about St. Gabriel visiting Our Lady and the time of the Annunciation, and then anything in the Creed that has to do with our Lord's Incarnation, which therefore also touches on Our Lady's Immaculate Conception. So anything that is said about the elevation of human nature *above* its natural place *below* the angelic order is what the demons just despise. This is because Our Lady's Immaculate Conception is one that elevates, that catapults, us above the angels, and therefore above the demons, so they hate that, they hate her Immaculate Conception. Further, our own humanity being taken up by the Word in the Incarnation and Our Lady's role in that, the fact that He took His flesh from her—they just hate all of that, and I think it's precisely because of the elevation of the dignity of humanity above that of the angelic order.

Have you seen indicators that the demons hate the Hail Mary prayer?

Fr. Lampert: Oh, absolutely. You think of the Hail Mary prayer—it's the words of the Archangel Gabriel to Mary, which is the Incarnation. The demons are infuriated by that because now human flesh is being elevated higher than themselves. Most people talk about the sin of pride as the fall of Lucifer, but it does seem that the angels were permitted to see a glimpse of God's plan for the Incarnation, that God would take on human form. The devil wanted God to unite His nature with the angelic nature. Lucifer wanted that to be him. God chose to take on human flesh, the Incarnation, and then human flesh is elevated higher than himself. Think of our Blessed Mother: she becomes Queen of Heaven, Queen of the Angels, and she's elevated higher than Lucifer, due to the rejection of the Incarnation. So the Hail Mary prayer, I think, speaks to the Incarnation, and I would expect that it would cause a strong negative reaction.

Experiences of the Exorcists

Do you think a person who was aided in an exorcism by, for example, Pope St. John Paul II would have a greater devotion to him afterward?

Fr. Lampert: Not necessarily, because sometimes when people are possessed, they have no recollection of what took place. Other people will say that once the demon manifests in their body, they're aware of what's taking place, but they're powerless to stop it. It's almost like they're a spectator in their own body. I would say that for the people who are aware of what's going on, I've seen them develop more of a devotion, but if they're oblivious to what's going on, then that would not be the case.

What purpose do the other (minor) elements, like the use of holy water and the Litany of the Saints, have in the Rite of Exorcism?

Fr. Lampert: The elements of the rite are meant to force the demon to reveal itself. Demons would prefer to remain hidden, but parts of the rite are basically dragging the demon out into the spotlight, if you will. Then once the demon reveals itself, then the battle against it begins. The first thing done is a blessing of the person with holy water, reminding them of our new life in Christ. And then demons react. Again, these are truths that they've rejected, all of these things that the Church is throwing in their faces, the things that they've rejected—in doing so, the demons will begin to lash out. So whether it's the blessing with holy water, the litany, it's forcing the demons to react.

What can you say about the issue of demons having a saint who is their "nemesis"? Is this something we can look into as an aid in our spiritual life?

Fr. Pius: In the exorcisms that I worked on, regarding the specific demons who were possessing the demoniacs, it would make a certain kind of sense, both with the possessed person's life but then, mysteriously, also with the priest-exorcist's life and the whole group of people in the deliverance ministry team.

There is a logic to why certain demons show up in certain people's lives even by way of possession. The logic is not usually given to us to understand. It's a demonic aping of God's plan, and there is this inverse logic and an inverse hierarchical arrangement that the demonic world operates on. One of the great exorcists in the country, from whom I have received a lot of help and training, who has a particular kind of spiritual insight, has paired me with certain demoniacs, essentially matching me with them based on this insight he has.

This senior priest has told me a couple stories that illustrate how all of this remains very mysterious, which I have also seen in my own priestly work. He told me about Lucifer himself, the prince of the whole demonic underworld, showing up in an exorcism involving a person you would not think would be so important to the demonic. You would think Lucifer would be a demon who would be possessing someone like a priest or someone in a powerful position. This arrangement doesn't seem to make any sense, but the logic behind it all is not given to us to understand exactly.

Have any angels ever shown up in your exorcisms?

Fr. Lampert: Only through the Litany of the Saints, because the angels are a part of that. During the exorcism, you just know, by invoking them, that they're present. It's not like you have to see them or anything like that. You just know that they're there.

You said you had an interesting experience where your guardian angel helped one of your energumen. Would you share it?

Fr. Timothy: So I got a call from one of my spiritual directees, an energumen, screaming that she was being assaulted by the demons. I simply turned to my guardian angel and said, "Go to her now," at which point I heard screaming on the phone, and she said, "Your guardian angel is here fighting with my guardian angel. They're fighting off the demons. I'm free. I'm safe. Thank you."

How do the demons try to distract you during exorcisms, and how does the presence of the Communion of Saints counteract this?

Fr. Alphonsus: I love how, in the rite, the instructions indicate that the exorcist should not pray in haste or with great emotion. I always love how some of our exorcists pray with great calmness, great ease, and great peace, not frantically or emotionally. Demons want to trigger our emotions, so we need to be on guard against that. Often, in the exorcism, we will be aware that demons are present in the room with us. The demon in the possessed person will often indicate this, even looking in a particular spot to indicate the demon is present there. Or they will be yelling and screaming or whatever. Again, this is often done primarily to unnerve us and distract us or cause us to give into fear and lose our trust in the Lord.

What we have to remember is that, while, yes, there are demons there, there are far more angels present in the room. Every one of us has an angel with us who is present and much more powerful than the demons. This, of course, is in addition to God Himself, and Our Lady, and all the saints—so I don't have any fear.

Could you explain the way in which you discern whether the demons are telling the truth about seeing a saint during an exorcism?

Fr. Pius: With all things in these times of prayer together, we take all of the things the demons say, like when they say they see a saint in the room, with a grain of salt. Demons are great liars, you know, and you never really know what manipulation is there in their words. They are so much smarter than we are.

So there's a kind of intuition that that person or that demon is experiencing the presence of some saint in the room. There is a kind of priestly intuition that happens at those times, where the priest makes the observation, like, "Okay, that demon really is tormented right now and really hates this saint and is seeing him in the room right now." However, there's always the danger that they're saying that to manipulate the people who are praying in the room in some way.

Fr. Timothy: Of course, I don't trust them when they speak, not until the last minute, or when they name something very accurate. As we know, all they want to do is lie and distract, so I don't trust anything they say until about the last five minutes or so before they leave.

Have you found the St. Benedict medal to be useful in exorcisms?

Fr. Szada: St. Benedict is very, very powerful in terms of driving out demons. We always—I always insist that people have St. Benedict medals with them, on them, around their house. St. Benedict, because of his experiences with demons, is very, very powerful, especially in terms of a follow-up session after a person has been freed.

Have you had a strong reaction from an energumen simply from the use of holy water?

Fr. Szada: I had the case one time where we were interviewing a woman, and I blessed her with holy water afterward. She jumped up and said, "What was that, that stung! What did you do?" She then said, "I've been blessed with holy water lots of times, but that's the first time I ever experienced anything like that." It was the first time she was ever blessed with holy water with blessed salt, and then she reacted to it—wow!

Exorcists are often saying that it is taking longer to cast out demons than it used to. Has that been your experience?

Fr. Szada: To be honest with you, freeing somebody very quickly is a rare thing these days. It usually requires multiple sessions in order to free somebody, because the people that are coming to you are not necessarily people who are faithful people, who are seeking help, but usually people who have dabbled in the occult or who don't really go to church.

How do you understand this modern difficulty?

Fr. Szada: Somebody put it this way, and I thought it was rather fascinating: when the priest stands in as the exorcist and does the ritual, as Fr. Amorth used to say, he could do the ritual once and the demons would be driven out because the priest isn't standing there on his own, he's standing there with the whole faith of the Church, the Mystical Body, behind him, angels and saints, as well as the whole Mystical Body of the pilgrim Church on earth. As faith has collapsed across the board in this world, the priest doesn't have the backing anymore that he used to have.

Practices of the Exorcists

Did you ever invoke any Blesseds or Venerables, or did you tend to stick with the saints?

Fr. Pius: I tended to stick with the saints unless there were some reason for me to do otherwise, such as because of the liturgical calendar or because of the demoniac's personal life. There was one family who was involved rather closely with Opus Dei, and at that point I don't think Jose Maria Escriva was a saint, but I invoked his assistance. So if there is a family connection of some sort, we would invoke the Blesseds or Venerables.

What are sources you look to in order to decide which saints to invoke?

Fr. Athanasius: It is helpful to invoke the saint of the day, the possessed person's Confirmation saint, saints of their particular devotion, and even the saints that they were reading about and invoking in their spiritual life at the time.

How important is it that the exorcist knows the relics he is using are authentic?

From Fr. Girolamo Menghi, OFM: The exorcist should also be cautious in the application of sensible objects, such as sacred relics. He should take the utmost care to ensure that they are, in fact, genuine holy articles, whether they be relics of saints, or fragments of the true cross, or other such items. He should take this caution both for his own sake, and for the sake of other persons who are present, and only use such articles if he is confidently assured of their authenticity. For demons will often pretend to be in fear of such items, when they know perfectly well that they are not genuine at all. And afterwards, they will then mock or treat scornfully the non-genuine sacred article. They do this in order to undermine people's faith in the sacraments and piety of the holy Roman Church. I myself have sometimes witnessed this very thing occur in astonishing fashion.[348]

Cautions about Curiosity and Revelations

How is the appearance of the saints different from a private revelation or mystical encounter?

Fr. Athanasius: When the saints are involved, it is not that they "appear," it is not something that I see, but something the demons see. It is not like a running commentary from a saint is being given. I am not looking for any insights or "revelations" from the saints—I don't want that! The important and necessary things are grace, prayer, and virtue, not learning and knowledge.

When sensing the presence of the saints, it is not about receiving hidden knowledge or anything like that. Would you agree?

Fr. Timothy: Absolutely. In my experiences, I have noted the sense of discretion, almost modesty, on the part of the saints, almost like they are saying, "I don't even want my name mentioned." I have found that, for example, St. Philomena is very discreet and modest, such that we're not even notified of her presence and her assistance is not even acknowledged. She seems to want it

---

[348] Menghi, *The Scourge of Demons*, 30.

that way so my eyes are always directed toward Jesus. She appears to be saying, "Yes, I am here, but keep your focus on my Savior."

What is your reaction when demons speak or try to tell you something?

Fr. Lampert: Over the years, I don't really pay attention to demons. They may be telling a lie. They may be telling the truth, but I don't want to use the demon as the source of what I believe or don't believe. I don't think that that's the best teacher to have.

Have you ever had the demon start complaining about the presence of a saint?

Fr. Szada: I don't go there, usually I make them be silent.

Have the saints ever provided any sort of clarification of spiritual truths?

Fr. Szada: I hear what you're saying but we have to be very careful. Sometimes, a priest will get off track and ask a question of a demon that he should not ask. I saw one case where the senior exorcist jumped in to stop the younger priest, saying, "No, no, you can't go there!" This can happen. When it does, it must be stopped immediately, because that's when demons begin to take advantage of it. This is why I personally tend to stick to the ritual. I focus on the ritual and not all that other stuff. All the other stuff can become a distraction; stick to the rite. Stick to the ritual. Obviously, you have to be somewhat flexible, dealing with the situation, but don't allow yourself to be tempted.

Learning from the Saints

What is the greatest thing that the saints have taught you?

Fr. Pius: I think that the saints have become very, very dear to me in a way that they weren't before. This is a function of my age, a function of religious life, and a function of the priesthood. They help me to remember (and I wish everybody in the Church would remember) that the Christian life is more about doing good than it is about avoiding evil. That would be my parting thought, especially when you're writing a book about exorcism and deliverance ministry. The saints help remind us of that.

I tend to encourage people, when they think about their spiritual lives and spiritual warfare, to remember (and this is a very important thing) that we're already victorious, we're already saved, we're already washed in the Precious Blood of Christ; we already share in His victory, so we don't have anything to be afraid of, really. Rather than seeing ourselves as somehow doomed to failure and just barely protected by their grace and protection, we are gradually watching ourselves, through God's grace, become more and more like God. We're watching our divinization unfold through their protection and intercession. So I like that more positive slant to it.

You said the saints present a strong counter-message to Satan's accusations about our guilt. Can you explain?

Fr. Lampert: The key ingredient in that is to be able to repent, if we're ready to repent. I think the saints teach us that God's always ready to forgive. You think of the Book of Revelation chapter 3 verse 20, "he stands at the door and knocks." We have to open the door and let Him in, and the saints tell us that one of the ways that we can let Him in is simply by repenting. You go back to the book of Genesis when Adam and Eve sinned, and they went and hid. God is the one who moves through the garden and says, "Adam where are you?" But God knew where he was physically, that he was hiding, but he's trying to get Adam to admit that he's in a state of sin: "Where are you?" … "In a state of sin." If Adam can admit that and repent, God would forgive. I think saints always echo that message, but again Satan, these demons, would say, "No, you sinned, strike one, you're out."

Certain Saints to Invoke

What are the best spiritual aids for causing demons to scatter?

Fr. Lampert: Certainly, at the top of that list would be our Blessed Mother. I tell people there are three things that cause demons to flee: the Holy Name of Jesus, the Blood of Jesus, and the intercession of our Blessed Mother, the Queen of the Angels, the Queen of Heaven, the Queen of the Saints.

Do you have any recommendations for people on how they can make use of invoking Mary under different titles, or through different prayers, in order to find help in times of temptation?

Fr. Pius: St. Bernard has a beautiful homily about the holy name of Mary, about calling upon Mary, invoking her name, the actual name itself, *Mary*, like *Jesus*, is a powerful protection and help in times of temptation. So if someone is praying, and praying *through the names of Jesus and Mary* while they're being tempted, it's impossible that they will sin. If we're calling upon the name of Mary in a time of temptation, we will not sin. I remember when

I was in high school, a priest recommended to pray three Hail Marys before going to bed, for purity of mind, purity of heart, and purity of body. I remember that, and I practiced that for a lot of my young adulthood. That's basically using Our Lady's name to protect us from temptation, from the incursions of the enemy, of the devil. I think people will have, in their own devotional life, some affinity or affection for particular titles of Our Lady: "gate of heaven," "morning star," "Our Lady of Sorrows," as you suggested. A lot of that has to do with our own personal lives, and maybe what we need most in our life, and also our temperament, our struggles, our personality. The beautiful thing about the invocations of the titles of Our Lady is that they can morph to fit every situation or any situation. Someone might love the title of "mystical rose"—if that person loves that title, then that's going to be the most powerful thing they can invoke in times of temptation because it's close to them, it's important to them; they love Our Lady *in this way* and she'll be present to them *in this way*.

A devotional practice of Mother Teresa of Calcutta was that whenever she was really in a pickle, or in a real and seemingly impossible situation, she would recite nine times the Memorare,[349] like a little novena. The Memorare was written by St. Bernard of Clairvaux. That's a great idea, and I've used that in my own life. I think that's one of those that shows there's not like a "catch all" or trick or something like that, but these ancient prayers

---

[349] Remember, O most gracious Virgin Mary, that never was it known that anyone who fled to thy protection, implored thy help, or sought thine intercession was left unaided. Inspired by this confidence, I fly unto thee, O Virgin of virgins, my mother; to thee do I come, before thee I stand, sinful and sorrowful. O Mother of the Word Incarnate, despise not my petitions, but in thy mercy hear and answer me. Amen.

that were written by saints and prayed with faith—that's the way forward. The most ancient prayer to Our Lady is the *Sub Tuum Praesidium*—"We fly to thy patronage, O holy Mother of God."[350] Most Catholics don't know that prayer. I pray it in Latin every time I get in the car; that's a very powerful prayer because of its antiquity and because it's been prayed by Christians for sixteen or seventeen hundred years.

Devotions for the Faithful

What are some good devotions to the saints that the faithful could take up?

Fr. Pius: I think staying with the devotional actions of the Church as she presents them to us liturgically or para-liturgically is the best way. There are the great litanies that the Church blesses with indulgences when praying them publicly: the Litany of the Saints, the Litany of the Sacred Heart, the Litany of the Precious Blood, the Litany of St. Joseph, the Litany of Our Lady—obviously those are the supreme ones. All of the devotions are to help us with the intimate connection and spiritual fortification that we find in these relationships with these members of the Church in Heaven. However we go about that is just fine; there's no wrong way to do that. So if someone likes to meditate contemplatively on a particular litany or particular devotion after Mass, great!—if that's

---

[350] We fly to thy patronage, O holy Mother of God; despise not our petitions in our necessities, but deliver us always from all dangers, O glorious and blessed Virgin. Amen. In Latin: *Sub tuum praesidium confugimus, Sancta Dei Genetrix. Nostras deprecationes ne despicias in necessitatibus, sed a periculis cunctis libera nos semper, Virgo gloriosa et benedicta. Amen.*

helping their devotional life and drawing them closer to God and the angels and saints. There's almost no wrong way to do that. The Church shows us the ones that she prefers, but that doesn't mean that those need to eclipse any others that come from our own devotional life. Letting the Church guide us with the wisdom of her tradition and liturgy is always the best way forward, and then that opens up room for more personal kinds of devotions.

What are your thoughts on the power of being in the presence of a relic, in our home[351] or in our parish church, or even putting sacramentals in our home?

Fr. Pius: I can't recommend all of that enough. This reminds us in tangible, concrete ways of the Incarnational reality of our holy religion. It helps us restore that sacramental worldview that I was talking about before. It is the antidote to modernity, to materialism, to post-modernity, to Protestantism, and to the Enlightenment: all of the errors that ruin our Catholic faith and devotional lives. All of these things help us remember the reality that the world is an interpenetration of the spiritual and the material, just like our bodies, which are souls and bodies. Our

---

[351] On having relics in a home, Fr. Pius said, "The discipline of the church is that they're kept in holy places for public veneration. The Church wants the public veneration of her relics ... but in this day and age, and so many of them are just peddled on eBay and or ignored in a church closet and never loved or venerated or even seen, well then, it's better having it sitting on somebody's home altar and loved and venerated and kept firmly in mind than either sold on eBay or hidden away in some closet in the sacristy. So we have to just do the best we can with the circumstances that we live in, in these latter days of cooling devotion to these material things."

Lord became Incarnate in that way. Our bodies are going to rise from the dead—*these* bodies, these very ones.

Post-modernity doesn't make it easy for us to believe that or to remember that, so all of these things, all of these sacramentals, like St. Benedict medals, but even better, relics, are here to point us back to the Sacrament of the Church where we touch, concretely, the humanity of Our Lord and Savior Jesus Christ.

So I just can't recommend all of these things enough, beginning with holy images, but then extended to sacramentals that are blessed by the Church, to the relics of the saints, to visiting cemeteries and praying for the dead. All of this is about restoring this authentic Christian worldview which, the farther away we get from Our Lord's Ascension into Heaven, the easier it is for us to lose. The world is growing cold in sin until Christ comes again in glory, and so we have to strive, we must strive, to keep these truths firmly in mind. That's what all of these material things help us to do. The collateral of that is that, of course, it keeps demons far away—they hate all of it.

What are some ways that parents can protect their children from the diabolical?

Fr. Benedict: Fathers, in particular, and mothers should bless their children every single day with their fatherly, motherly blessing. And in the *Book of Blessings* for the Catholic Church, that was the only blessing included that lay people can do. A parent also has a priestly blessing—equivalent of a priest blessing, mothers and fathers have for their own natural or adopted children. You would be surprised how many parishes never talk about this and how many parents do not know about this. We should bless our children every single day, even when they're going to college and out of the house and come home—give them your fatherly and motherly blessing. Fathers should be the priest of the family. And they should bless the house with holy water seven nights of the week, not once a year, not once a month. But it's good to bless the house every day. And mother and father can take turns. And to bless every room, especially the bedrooms of the children. In our day and age, it's wise to do it seven days of the week. It doesn't need to be something long. It can be done easily in one or two or three minutes. Every Catholic house should have the St. Benedict Medal planted in the property around it.[352] It is also wise to have a St. Benedict Medal really in every room above the door. It is also wise to have every member of the family wear a medal.

Exorcists emphasize the Church's tradition that fathers can and should bless their children. Could they do so using a relic?

Fr. Pius: A father can bless his children, and why not use those holy objects to do that.

Do you think the faithful should begin taking up the Litany of the Saints as a regular devotion?

Fr. Lampert: I would agree. I think that's a particular prayer that is not in common practice but is very powerful. You could even think of the Divine Praises, which speak of God and speak of Mary and St. Joseph. Those things are very powerful. The fact that a lot of Catholics don't know some of these standard things is why, oftentimes, you might find Catholics getting bored with their Catholic Faith and believing they have to borrow and start doing

---

[352] The St. Benedict Medal is traditionally put in the four corners of the house or around the yard.

practices that are non-Christian, coming from eastern spiritualities. It's almost like, "They have something that we don't," but the reality is the Catholic Church has such a great treasury of prayers; we just have to really learn and tap into that. There are so many things out there that are underutilized simply because Catholics may not be as familiar; they may not even know about them.

Any practical advice on how one can grow in devotion to the saints?

Fr. Benedict: I think the best way to grow in devotion to the saints, and it is best if it begins when we are little children, is to read the lives of the saints. It is the absolute best way—to read actual biographies of them. It puts meat and bones on them. You can identify with them. People relate to stories.

What are some steps to becoming a saint, that is, to grow in holiness?

Fr. Benedict: There is a certain primacy to Eucharistic Adoration. I think even children and teenagers should go. I think more priests need to make Eucharistic holy hours. I think the number one source of grace is Eucharistic Adoration. Adoration is not disconnected—it's integrally united to the Mass. It flows from the Mass, and it leads us back to the Mass. John Paul II said one reason why every Catholic needs Adoration is because the grace received at Mass is so powerful and so overflowing you cannot possibly absorb it. You need Adoration to absorb what you just received. It's too much. So Adoration allows me to effectively absorb all the graces of the Liturgy. Of course, at the same time, it prepares me for my next Mass.

Appendix B

The Impact of the Saints
in the Life of an Exorcist

The power within the Rite of Exorcism is the same power that Our Lord Jesus Christ Himself wielded, albeit infinitely more powerfully, when He delivered people from bondage to the enemy. He then entrusted this power to His Apostles and to their successors and collaborators. Exorcists experience this reality through their work. As Pope St. John Paul II said after performing an exorcism, "Everything that happens in the Gospels still happens today."[353]

The work of exorcists brings them into a unique situation in which they are permitted, in limited ways, to "see behind the veil," to see what is happening in the invisible realms of the spiritual world. Msgr. Rossetti said, "One of the great graces we receive in our ministry is a personal experience of the truths of the Catholic Faith."[354] Fr. Alphonsus concurred, stating, "We can clearly recognize the power of the Lord and the love of Our Lady and her power, as well as the saints."[355]

---

[353] The editors of Sophia Institute Press, *The Pope's Exorcist*, 75.

[354] Rossetti, *Diary of an American Exorcist*, 255.

[355] Fr. Alphonsus, in discussion with Charles D. Fraune, August 2024.

"In an exorcism, we enter the supernatural realm of the angels and saints,"[356] Msgr. Rossetti said, adding, "In those sessions, we experience firsthand the powerful Communion of Saints. These holy men and women are with us, helping us in our lives and ministries, including helping us cast out demons."[357] Fr. Ripperger said that he is often asked, "What is the most bizarre and fascinating thing you've seen?" He explained, "I just say, 'Look, demons are boring; they do the same stuff over and over again. What's interesting is what you hear about Our Lord and Our Lady or some saint.'"[358]

For some exorcists, it was only through this ministry that their eyes were finally opened to the reality of the Church's teaching about the intercessory power of the saints. Fr. Alphonsus admitted to this, saying,

Yes, and I hate to admit it but, even though I have been a priest for many decades, it has only been through this ministry that the intercession of the saints has become a much more concrete and objective reality. I have much more awareness now, and therefore I call upon the saints much more than I did beforehand. In seminary, we weren't really taught to do that. I mean, the saints were briefly gone over in our formation, but, just like with your guardian angel, there wasn't an emphasis on really having a *relationship* with your guardian angel or really seeking to have a *relationship* with the saints. It's kind of like, yeah, we pray, we ask the saints to pray for us at certain times of the year and in the liturgy, but it wasn't that there was

356 Rossetti, *Diary of an American Exorcist*, 175.
357 Ibid., 255.
358 Ripperger, "Our Lady of Sorrows and Healing."

an encouragement or a teaching that, "Hey, you should really have these relationships with your patron saints," ones you choose and ones who choose you. That's something I've only come to really see particularly through this ministry.[359]

Fr. Alphonsus said that now, when a particular saint makes his presence known in an exorcism, he knows that not only is this a saint that the possessed person needs to be calling upon but that this is a saint that he himself needs to seek assistance from while ministering to this particular person.[360] It is in examples like this that we see that a devotion to a saint is often chosen by the saint, not by the individual on earth.

Once his attention was captured by the saints, his understanding of their presence began to grow, Fr. Alphonsus explained. "In particular, for me, St. Charbel has been present in my life," he said, adding,

> Then, every year, it just seems like more saints, of a variety of kinds, have become more present. That encourages me, in times of stress or strain, to appeal to them. I've seen how difficulties and other situations just resolve, how the anxiety dissipates, and my trust in the Lord grows, and the intercessory power of the saints grow stronger. So, yes, I have definitely been seeing that.[361]

Fr. Timothy echoed this new understanding. He said, "My experience is that I've been encircled with the saints, almost always. For example, today is the feast of a martyr from the French

[359] Fr. Alphonsus, in discussion with Charles D. Fraune, August 2024.
[360] Ibid.
[361] Ibid.

Revolution, and it is clear to me that he is with me all day. I'm very conscious of his presence, of having a martyr at my side."[362] As a result of his experiences, Fr. Timothy has greatly increased his study of the lives of the saints and now devotes part of each day to learning about them. He explained,

> This way, we can be more attentive to their presence and activity. Each day, I try to memorize all the saints whose feasts fall on that day. Through this, God has so blessed this study by giving me a heightened awareness of the saints and their intercessory presence at exorcisms and also in my daily life. It's a very joyful thing, and exciting, to be aware of all of these saints.[363]

Story: How a Saint Revealed Herself to an Exorcist

In our conversations with Fr. Timothy, he provided a powerful testimony of the mysterious ways in which the saints come to our aid:

> There's a story I like to tell: we have a very large bridge in our area. I was working with five people who were demonically possessed or obsessed[364] or suffering, on some level, from a demonic attachment, and they all had suicidal ideations. It was on the feast of St. Rita of

---

[362] Fr. Timothy, in discussion with Charles D. Fraune, August 2024.

[363] Ibid.

[364] Obsession is an internal diabolical assault involving a bombardment of thoughts into the person's mind, in which the demon attacks the person's imagination and emotions, often leading to an experience of visions, hearing voices, and hallucinating (see *Slaying Dragons*, 40).

Cascia, who's a personal friend of mine, and I was getting dressed for the day and thinking about all the people I needed to meet with that week when, as I recall, I had this experiential awareness of a being of light appearing on my right-hand side, as if through the window. It was a feminine voice that said, "Do not worry. I will care for her. She will not jump from the bridge," and, with a smile, this feminine person disappeared. Well, my first thought was, "That was St. Rita of Cascia because it's her feast day!" Quickly, though, the Holy Spirit said to me, "No, it's St. Mary Magdalene de Pazzi." That wasn't the most familiar saint to me at the time, but I remembered that, two years prior, I had visited her tomb, where she is incorrupt. Further, her feast day, May 24, was that Saturday, the day the woman was going to jump from the bridge. Further still, I had no idea that she is the patron saint of those who cut themselves, those who have suicidal ideations, and those who have been possessed by demons. So that is one way in which I have had a real active sense of a connection with the saints.[365]

The Saints' Impact

When Fr. Pius explained the impact of working as an exorcist, his answer was so eloquent that we decided to quote him in full here. He explains how we must work to remember and to maintain an active awareness that we are members of the Mystical Body of Christ, a Body that includes the angels and the saints who have entered into their eternal glory. The "sacramental worldview"

[365] Fr. Timothy, in discussion with Charles D. Fraune, August 2024.

that the Church provides is the perspective that we must seek in order to remember these sacred realities well:

> I think that working in the world of exorcism for the time that I did, as well as deliverance ministry, helped me with a restoration, or a deepening, of what I'll call a "sacramental worldview," an authentically Catholic, pre-modern worldview. In a certain respect, I wish that every Catholic could witness the Major Rite of Exorcism. Obviously, the Church doesn't recommend that, and for a number of good reasons, but what you see there, so vividly before your eyes, is the power of the evil one, the power of the Sacraments of the Church, and the power of the intercession of the saints.
>
> It's obvious how we *ought* to think about life, but we forget because we're with creatures all the time. So my worldview: very often, as a Religious, I spend a lot of the day praying the Psalms, praying the Divine Liturgy, the sacred liturgy. I very often think of us, as human creatures in the choir stalls, or in the nave of the Church, living members of the Church, being here praying; and I imagine us being surrounded by this cloud of witnesses who are really present. Let's consider the saint of the day, the saints whom we're commemorating or invoking or recalling or whose patronage we live under, and the angels, then, all around; this sort of hierarchical arrangement of souls: our own, the saints, the angels, and Almighty God. I very often think about that throughout the day, not just when I'm in Church praying but also as I'm going about my day, remembering that I'm surrounded, I'm accompanied, by my guardian angel; I'm surrounded by the saints, who are

my patrons, who have this special friendship and affection for me, personally, who are with me. I'm thinking that this world is permeated, penetrated, interpenetrated, with these real presences of real persons—that has definitely changed since my work in the world of exorcism and deliverance ministry.

I try to remember—though, as a weak man, I often forget—so I must let the Church and let the saints and angels remind me of their tangible presence with me. I wish more Catholics would live like that. In a way, it's a medieval worldview, one that we lost with the advent of modernity in the Enlightenment. A medieval person, for example, would look at a tree outside, maybe it's an apple tree, and they would remember the Cross, they would think of Adam buried at the foot of the Cross, they would think of that being the instrument of their salvation; all of that would be an instinct every time they saw a piece of wood. We modern people don't really have that worldview anymore, but the devotion to the saints can help us restore it because that's the real worldview. Why is there a tree outside my window? It's not just by pure chance, but so that I can remember the higher order of reality, which is the sacramental worldview.[366]

---

[366] Fr. Pius, in discussion with Patrick O'Hearn, September 2024.

An Overview of the Rite of Exorcism

A summary of the text of the Rite of Exorcism

Once the priest is properly prepared, by going to Confession and offering devout prayers (including Holy Mass, if time and circumstances allow), the priest, vested in surplice and stole, in the presence of the possessed, traces the sign of the cross over the possessed, himself, and any bystanders.

He then sprinkles the possessed with holy water, kneels down, and prays the Litany of the Saints.

He then proceeds to ask God to banish the demon from the possessed person and commands the demon to depart. Immediately afterward, he recites the prologue of the Gospel of St. John, in which the Incarnation of the Son of God, who came into the world to destroy the power of the devil, is proclaimed against the devil and his efforts to destroy human souls. He then, further, reads from places in the Gospel in which Our Lord bestows upon His priests the power to cast out the devil (e.g., Mark 16:15–18; Luke 10:17–20; Luke 11:14–22).

The priest asks Our Lord to "bestow upon [him] steadfast faith and the power to attack this cruel demon with assurance and fearlessness, fortified by the might of Thy holy arm."

He then proceeds with the authoritative commands that the demon depart from the possessed. It is recommended that the exorcist repeat these lengthy commands until the person is liberated.

It is also deemed "very helpful" for the priest "to say devoutly over and over again" the Our Father, the Hail Mary, and the Creed, in addition to other prayers and psalms that are provided in the rite.

Appendix D

Resources for Continued Growth

Spiritual Warfare

Deliverance Prayers: For Use by the Laity, by Fr. Chad Ripperger, includes powerful prayers from the public domain and the Church's treasury for the laity to wage spiritual warfare. (Sentrad press.com)

Diary of an American Exorcist: Demons, Possession, and the Modern-Day Battle against Ancient Evil, by Msgr. Stephen J. Rossetti, describes the healing power of Christ for the possessed and for the exorcist and reveals amazing moments when Christ and His Church visibly triumph over Satan. (SophiaInstitute.com)

Exorcism: The Battle against Satan and His Demons, by Fr. Vincent Lampert, equips Catholics with the knowledge necessary to avoid becoming vulnerable to spiritual attacks. (StPaulcenter.com)

The Rise of the Occult: What Exorcists and Former Occultists Want You to Know, by Charles D. Fraune, is based on forty interviews and extensive research. Fraune follows the real experiences of those who have been involved in the occult and exposes its reality in our world today. (SlayingDragonsPress.com)

The Occult among Us: Exorcists and Former Occultists Expose the Nature of this Modern Evil, by Charles D. Fraune, is based on the same interviews in *The Rise of the Occult* and addresses over twenty different critical topics related to the spiritual war playing out in our world. (SlayingDragonsPress.com)

The Scourge of Demons, by Fr. Girolamo Menghi, OFM, the "Father of the Exorcist's Art," is a sixteenth-century classic manual on exorcisms that was popular with priests and laity throughout Europe. (SlayingDragonsPress.com)

Slaying Dragons: What Exorcists See & What We Should Know, by Charles D. Fraune, has become a modern spiritual warfare classic, presenting the teachings of modern exorcists, great saints, and Doctors of the Church to explain all the basics of spiritual warfare and the pursuit of holiness that Catholics today need to know. (SlayingDragonsPress.com)

Swords and Shadows: Navigating Youth Amidst the Wiles of Satan, by Charles D. Fraune, presents the wisdom of *Slaying Dragons* to the youth of our culture, in the context of the author's youth and conversion, to help teenagers and their parents navigate this fallen world. (SlayingDragonsPress.com)

Spiritual Warfare and the Discernment of Spirits, by Dan Burke, gives a foundational understanding of the battleground of the mind, how the enemy works in this area, and how Scripture and the wisdom of St. Ignatius of Loyola can help you fight back against the world, the flesh, and the devil—and win. (SpiritualDirection.com/shop)

The Exorcism Files: True Stories of Demonic Possession and *The History of Exorcism*, by Adam Blai, are two wonderful books that dive deeper into the topic of exorcisms, especially the signs of diabolical possessions. (SophiaInstitute.com)

The Liber Christo Method: A Field Manual for Spiritual Combat, by Dr. Dan Schneider, is a protocol developed by Doloran Fathers to assist those suffering from or assisting in the fight against diabolical oppression. (TanBooks.com)

Marian Devotion

Our Lady of Sorrows: Devotion to Mary's Seven Sorrows for Children, by Patrick O'Hearn, is a children's book with meditations and prayers to console Mary in her Seven Sorrows; the book includes four original prayers by Fr. Chad Ripperger. (SophiaInstitute.com)

The Virgin Mary and the Devil in Exorcisms, by Fr. Francesco Bamonte, reveals the powerful role of Mary in the spiritual battle, especially in exorcisms. (PopeLeo13institute.org)

Saints

Parents of the Saints: The Hidden Heroes Behind Our Favorite Saints, by Patrick O'Hearn, highlights the seven hallmarks of godly parents through the lives of fifty holy couples. (TanBooks.com)

Prayer

Prayer into the Deep: Finding Peace through Prayer, by Dan Burke, is the simplest, most straightforward book in print on how to begin or deepen your prayer life. (SpiritualDirection.com/shop)

Come Away by Yourselves: A Guide to Prayer for Busy Catholics, by Charles D. Fraune, based on a classic work of St. Alphonsus Liguori, guides the reader along a practical route for bringing retreat-depth prayer into a perpetually busy daily routine. (SlayingDragonsPress.com)

Stones of St. Michael

To obtain a stone from the Shrine Basilica of St. Michael the Archangel in Gargano, Italy, you can make a donation at this website: https://www.santuariosanmichele.it/. This donation will cover the cost of shipping and the reliquary. Please note: this is not a "relic" in a traditional sense, so it can be purchased.

Prayers for Continued Growth

LITANY OF THE SAINTS[367]

Lord, have mercy on us.
Christ, have mercy on us.
Lord, have mercy on us.
Christ, hear us,
Christ, graciously hear us.

God, the Father of Heaven, have mercy on us.
God the Son, Redeemer of the world, have mercy on us.
God, the Holy Spirit, have mercy on us.
Holy Trinity, One God, have mercy on us.

Holy Mary, pray for us.
Holy Mother of God, pray for us.
Holy Virgin of virgins, pray for us.

St. Michael, pray for us.
St. Gabriel, pray for us.
St. Raphael, pray for us.
All ye holy angels and archangels, pray for us.
All ye holy orders of blessed spirits, pray for us.

---

[367] From *The Roman Ritual*, vol. 2, 453.

St. John the Baptist, pray for us.
St. Joseph, pray for us.
All ye holy patriarchs and prophets, pray for us.

St. Peter, pray for us.
St. Paul, pray for us.
St. Andrew, pray for us.
St. James, pray for us.
St. John, pray for us.
St. Thomas, pray for us.
St. James, pray for us.
St. Philip, pray for us.
St. Bartholomew, pray for us.
St. Matthew, pray for us.
St. Simon, pray for us.
St. Thaddeus, pray for us.
St. Matthias, pray for us.
St. Barnabas, pray for us.
St. Luke, pray for us.
St. Mark, pray for us.
All ye holy apostles and evangelists, pray for us.
All ye holy disciples of our Lord, pray for us.

All ye Holy Innocents, pray for us.
St. Stephen, pray for us.
St. Lawrence, pray for us.
St. Vincent, pray for us.
Sts. Fabian and Sebastian, pray for us.
Sts. John and Paul, pray for us.
Sts. Cosmas and Damian, pray for us.
Sts. Gervase and Protase, pray for us.
All ye holy martyrs, pray for us.

St. Sylvester, pray for us.
St. Gregory, pray for us.
St. Ambrose, pray for us.
St. Augustine, pray for us.
St. Jerome, pray for us.
St. Martin, pray for us.
St. Nicholas, pray for us.
All ye holy bishops and confessors, pray for us.
All ye holy doctors, pray for us.

St. Anthony, pray for us.
St. Benedict, pray for us.
St. Bernard, pray for us.
St. Dominic, pray for us.
St. Francis, pray for us.
All ye holy priests and Levites, pray for us.
All ye holy monks and hermits, pray for us.

St. Mary Magdalene, pray for us.
St. Agatha, pray for us.
St. Lucy, pray for us.
St. Agnes, pray for us.
St. Cecilia, pray for us.
St. Catherine, pray for us.
St. Anastasia, pray for us.
All ye holy virgins and widows, pray for us.
All ye holy men and women, saints of God,
    make intercession for us.

Be merciful, spare us, O Lord.
Be merciful, graciously hear us, O Lord.

From all evil, O Lord, deliver us.

From all sin, O Lord, deliver us.
From Thy wrath, O Lord, deliver us.
From a sudden and unprovided death, O Lord, deliver us.
From the snares of the devil, O Lord, deliver us.
From anger, and hatred, and all ill will, O Lord, deliver us.
From the spirit of fornication, O Lord, deliver us.
From lightning and tempest, O Lord, deliver us.
From the scourge of earthquake, O Lord, deliver us.
From pestilence, famine, and war, O Lord, deliver us.
From everlasting death, O Lord, deliver us.

Through the mystery of Thy holy Incarnation,
    O Lord, deliver us.
Through Thine Advent, O Lord, deliver us.
Through Thy Nativity, O Lord, deliver us.
Through Thy baptism and holy fasting, O Lord, deliver us.
Through Thy Cross and Passion, O Lord, deliver us.
Through Thy death and burial, O Lord, deliver us.
Through Thy holy Resurrection, O Lord, deliver us.
Through Thine admirable Ascension, O Lord, deliver us.
Through the coming of the Holy Spirit the Paraclete,
    O Lord, deliver us.
In the day of judgment, O Lord, deliver us.

We sinners, we beseech Thee, hear us,
That Thou wouldst spare us, we beseech Thee, hear us.
That Thou wouldst pardon us, we beseech Thee,
    hear us.
That Thou wouldst bring us to true penance,
    we beseech Thee, hear us.
That Thou wouldst govern and preserve Thy holy
    Church, we beseech Thee, hear us.

That Thou wouldst preserve our Apostolic Prelate, and
　　all ecclesiastical orders in holy religion, we beseech
　　Thee, hear us.
That Thou wouldst humble the enemies of Thy holy
　　Church, we beseech Thee, hear us.
That Thou wouldst give peace and true concord to
　　Christian kings and princes, we beseech Thee,
　　hear us.
That Thou wouldst grant peace and unity to all
　　Christian people, we beseech Thee, hear us.
That Thou wouldst bring back to the unity of the
　　Church all those who have strayed away, and lead to
　　the light of the Gospel all unbelievers, we beseech
　　Thee, hear us.
That Thou wouldst confirm and preserve us in Thy holy
　　service, we beseech Thee, hear us.
That Thou wouldst lift up our minds to heavenly
　　desires, we beseech Thee, hear us.
That Thou wouldst render eternal blessings to all our
　　benefactors, we beseech Thee, hear us.
That Thou wouldst deliver our souls, and the souls
　　of our brethren, relations, and benefactors, from
　　eternal damnation, we beseech Thee, hear us.
That Thou wouldst give and preserve the fruit of the
　　earth, we beseech Thee, hear us.
That Thou wouldst give eternal rest to all the faithful
　　departed, we beseech Thee, hear us.
That Thou wouldst graciously hear us, we beseech
　　Thee, hear us.
Son of God, we beseech Thee, hear us.

Lamb of God, who takest away the sins of the world,
spare us, O Lord.
Lamb of God, who takest away the sins of the world,
graciously hear us, O Lord.
Lamb of God, who takest away the sins of the world,
have mercy on us.

Christ, hear us.
Christ, graciously hear us.

Lord, have mercy on us.
Christ, have mercy on us.
Lord, have mercy on us.

CHAPLET OF ST. MICHAEL THE ARCHANGEL[368]

God, come to my assistance.
Lord, make haste to help me.
Glory be to the Father ...

---

[368] "Chaplet of Saint Michael," *Knights of the Holy Eucharist*, https://
www.knightsoftheholyeucharist.com/chaplet-of-saint-michael-
prayer-download/. The chaplet originates from a vision of St.
Michael to the Servant of God, Antonia d'Astonac, in which
the archangel told her that he should be honored through the
following devotion. This chaplet was approved by Pope Pius IX in
1851, and it can be found in the *Raccolta*, the traditional collection of indulgenced prayers. In the vision, St. Michael promised
that whoever would practice this devotion in his honor would
have, when approaching the Holy Table, an escort of nine angels
chosen from each of the nine choirs. In addition, for the daily
recital of these nine salutations, he promised his continual assistance as well as the assistance of all the holy angels during life;
and he promised deliverance from Purgatory for all who pray this
chaplet as well as for all their relations.

Pray one Our Father and three Hail Marys after each of the following nine salutations in honor of the nine choirs of angels.

By the intercession of St. Michael and the celestial Choir of Seraphim, may the Lord make us worthy to burn with the fire of perfect charity. Amen.

By the intercession of St. Michael and the celestial Choir of Cherubim, may the Lord grant us the grace to leave the ways of sin and run in the paths of Christian perfection. Amen.

By the intercession of St. Michael and the celestial Choir of Thrones, may the Lord infuse into our hearts a true and sincere spirit of humility. Amen.

By the intercession of St. Michael and the celestial Choir of Dominations, may the Lord give us grace to govern our senses and overcome any unruly passions. Amen.

By the intercession of St. Michael and the celestial Choir of Virtues, may the Lord preserve us from evil and falling into temptation. Amen.

By the intercession of St. Michael and the celestial Choir of Powers, may the Lord protect our souls against the snares and temptations of the devil. Amen.

By the intercession of St. Michael and the celestial Choir of Principalities, may God fill our souls with a true spirit of obedience. Amen.

By the intercession of St. Michael and the celestial Choir of Archangels, may the Lord give us perseverance in faith and in all good works in order that we may attain the glory of Heaven. Amen.

By the intercession of St. Michael and the celestial
    Choir of Angels, may the Lord grant us to be pro-
    tected by them in this mortal life and conducted in
    the life to come to Heaven. Amen.
*Pray one Our Father in honor of each angel: St. Michael, St. Gabriel,
St. Raphael, and our Guardian Angel.*

CLOSING PRAYERS

O glorious prince St. Michael, chief and commander of the heavenly hosts, guardian of souls, vanquisher of rebel spirits, servant in the house of the Divine King, and our admirable conductor, you who shine with excellence and superhuman virtue, deliver us from all evil, who turn to you with confidence; and enable us by your gracious protection to serve God more and more faithfully every day.

Pray for us, O glorious St. Michael, Prince of the
    Church of Jesus Christ,
That we may be made worthy of His promises.

Almighty and Everlasting God, who, by a prodigy of goodness and a merciful desire for the salvation of all men, has appointed the most glorious Archangel St. Michael Prince of Your Church, make us worthy, we ask You, to be delivered from all our enemies, that none of them may harass us at the hour of death, but that we may be conducted by him into Your Presence. This we ask through the merits of Jesus Christ Our Lord. *Amen.*

A Prayer to St. Antonino, Patron of Campagna, for Liberation from Evil Spirits[369]

Omnipotent and merciful God, You have granted to the Blessed St. Antonino, abbot, a special power against the devils; grant us we pray, that through his merits and his prayers, we may be liberated from their pitfalls and thus reach eternal life. We ask You through our Lord Jesus Christ, Your Son, who is God and lives and reigns with You in the unity of the Holy Spirit, forever and ever. Amen.

A Prayer by St. Mary of Jesus Crucified[370]

Holy Spirit, inspire me.
Love of God, consume me.
To the right path lead me.
Mary, my Mother, look down upon me.
With Jesus, bless me.
From all evil, all illusion, all danger, preserve me.

Anima Christi[371]

Soul of Christ, sanctify me.
Body of Christ, save me.
Blood of Christ, inebriate me.
Water from the side of Christ, wash me.
Passion of Christ, strengthen me.
O good Jesus, hear me.

---

[369] Amorth and Stanzione, *The Devil Is Afraid of Me*, 136.

[370] "Saint Mary of Jesus Crucified," *Carmelite Sisters of Ireland*, https://www.carmelitesisters.ie/blessed-mary-of-jesus-crucified-miriam-baouardy/.

[371] A fourteenth-century prayer popularized by St. Ignatius of Loyola.

Within Thy Wounds hide me.
Suffer me not to be separated from Thee.
From the malignant enemy, defend me.
In the hour of my death, call me,
And bid me to come to Thee.
That with Thy saints, I may praise Thee.
Forever and ever. Amen.

Prayer of St. Alphonsus Liguori[372]

Most holy Mary, Queen of Heaven, I who was once the slave of
the Evil One now dedicate myself to thy service forever; and I offer
myself to honor and to serve thee as long as I live. Accept me for
thy servant and cast me not away from thee as I deserve. In thee,
O my Mother, I place all my hope. All blessing and thanksgiving
be to God, who in His mercy giveth me this trust in thee. True
it is, that in past time I have fallen miserably into sin; but by the
merits of Jesus Christ, and by thy prayers, I hope that God has
pardoned me. But this is not enough, my Mother. One thought
appalls me: it is that I may yet lose the grace of God. Danger is
ever nigh; the devil sleeps not; fresh temptations assail me. Protect
me, then, my Queen; help me against the assaults of my spiritual
enemy. Never suffer me to sin again, or to offend Jesus, thy Son.
Let me not by sin lose my soul, Heaven, and my God. This one
grace, Mary, I ask of thee; this is my desire; this may thy prayers
obtain for me. Such is my hope. Amen. (Say three Hail Marys.)

---

[372] Ambrose St. John, *The Raccolta or Collection of Indulgenced Prayers
and Good Works* (New York: Benziger Bros., 1910), no. 185.

PRAYER OF BLESSING[373]

That the Lord Jesus may always be with you, walk before you in order to guide you, be behind you in order to protect you, dwell within you in order to keep you, be above you in order to enlighten you. Amen.

THE PRAYER OF A CHILD[374]

By St. Francis Xavier

A faithful Christian, when he is about to go to sleep, will keep all that has been said above by examining his conscience with respect to the sins he has committed during the day by resolving, with the grace of His Lord, to amend them, and by being determined to confess them when he can. And since sleep is the image of death, and many who have gone to sleep in good health are dead in the morning, I shall say the Confiteor with great repentance for my sins, and I shall commend myself to my holy guardian angel and pray as follows:

I, a sinner, who have wandered far astray, confess to the Lord God and to St. Mary and to St. Michael, the angel, and to St. John the Baptist . . . and to all the saints of the heavenly court . . . that I have sinned exceedingly through thought and through omission and through deed, that I did not do much good which I could have done, and that I did not refrain from much evil from which

---

[373] Amorth and Fezzi, *Father Amorth: My Battle against Satan*, 99. The following prayer was a blessing that Fr. Gabriele Amorth and Servant of God Fr. Candido Amantini used to give to each other.

[374] St. Francis Xavier, *The Letters and Instructions of Francis Xavier*, trans. M. Joseph Costelloe, S.J. (Brighton, MA: The Institute of Jesuit Sources, 1992); quoted in *Magnificat* 26, no. 10 (December 2024): 55–56.

I could have refrained, for all of which I am sorry.... I pray and ask my Lady, St. Mary, and all the saints that they may be willing to ask my Lord Jesus Christ that He may be willing to forgive me my present, past, confessed, and forgotten sins; and that from now on He may grant me His grace of keeping me from sinning and of bringing me to the enjoyment of the glory of paradise....

O blessed Cross that was sanctified by the Body of my Lord Jesus Christ and adorned with His precious Blood! I entreat You, merciful Lord Jesus Christ, through the efficacy of Your Passion and death, which You suffered on this most holy Cross, that You may deign to forgive me my sins as You forgave those of the thief when You, gracious Lord, hung crucified upon it, and that You may grant me victory over my adversaries and deign to bring my enemies to a knowledge of the truth so that they may repent.

Appendix F

Saintly Sayings

Men do not fear a powerful hostile army as the powers of
Hell fear the name and protection of Mary.

—St. Bonaventure[375]

In dangers of sinning, when assailed by temptations,
when doubtful as to how you should act, remember that
Mary can help you, and if you but call upon her, she will
instantly help you.

—St. Alphonsus Liguori[376]

Mary must be terrible to the devil and his crew, as an army
ranged in battle, principally in these latter times, because
the devil, knowing that he has but little time, and now
less than ever, to destroy souls, will every day redouble his
efforts and his combats. He will presently raise up cruel

---

[375] "Saint Quotes," Catholic Diocese of St. Petersburg, https://www
.dosp.org/our-faith/saints/saint-quotes/.

[376] Francis W. Johnston, *The Voices of the Saints: Counsels from the
Saints to Bring Comfort and Guidance in Daily Living* (Charlotte,
NC: Tan Books, 1986), 168.

persecutions and will put terrible snares before the faithful servants and true children of Mary, whom it gives him more trouble to conquer than it does to conquer others.

—St. Louis de Montfort[377]

After the Holy Eucharist, the Holy Rosary is the strongest weapon to fight the devil.

—St. Carlo Acutis[378]

The battle against the devil is the principal task of St. Michael the Archangel. And [it] is still being fought today.

—Pope St. John Paul II[379]

When I think of them [the saints], I feel myself inflamed by a tremendous yearning.... We long to share in the citizenship of Heaven, to dwell with the spirits of the blessed.

—St. Bernard of Clairvaux[380]

Therefore, says St. Thomas, it is good to have recourse to many saints, "because by the prayers of many we can sometimes obtain that which we cannot by the prayers of one."

—St. Alphonsus Liguori[381]

---

[377] St. Louis de Montfort, *True Devotion to Mary with Preparation for Total Consecration*, 22.

[378] Ferrisi, *Blessed Carlo Acutis*, 99.

[379] Pope St. John Paul II, May 24, 1987, during a visit to the Sanctuary of St. Michael the Archangel.

[380] Rossetti, *Diary of an American Exorcist*, 256.

[381] St. Alphonsus Liguori, *The Great Means of Salvation and of Perfection* (Brooklyn, NY: Redemptorist Fathers, 1927), 35.

Bibliography

"A Former Satanist Priest Who Became a Saint." *Dominican Friars Foundation.* https://dominicanfriars.org/former-satanist-priest-became-saint/.

Agasso, Domenico. *Fr. Gabriele Amorth: Rome's Exorcist.* Translated by Bret Thoman, OFS. Gastonia, NC: TAN Books, 2023.

Amorth, Fr. Gabriele. *An Exorcist Explains the Demonic: The Antics of Satan and His Army of Fallen Angels.* Translated by Charlotte J. Fasi. Manchester, NH: Sophia Institute Press, 2016.

Amorth, Fr. Gabriele. *Get Behind Me, Satan.* Translated by Nicholas Reitzug. Manchester, NH: Sophia Institute Press, 2023.

Amorth, Fr. Gabriele with Elisabetta Fezzi. *Father Amorth: My Battle against Satan.* Translated by Charlotte J. Fasi. Manchester, NH: Sophia Institute Press, 2018.

Amorth, Fr. Gabriele with Marcello Stanzione. *The Devil Is Afraid of Me: The Life and Works of the World's Most Famous Exorcist.* Translated by Charlotte J. Fasi. Manchester, NH: Sophia Institute Press, 2019.

Aquinas, St. Thomas. *The Summa Theologiae of St. Thomas Aquinas.* 2nd rev. ed. Translated by the Fathers of the English Dominican Province. 1920. Available at https://www.newadvent.org/summa/.

St. Athanasius. *St. Antony of the Desert.* Translated by Dom J. B. McLaughlin, O.S.B. Charlotte, NC: Tan Books, 2014.

Bamonte, Fr. Francesco. *The Virgin Mary and the Devil in Exorcisms.* 3rd English ed. Milan, Italy: Paoline, 2014.

Blai, Adam. *The Catholic Guide to Miracles: Separating the Authentic from the Counterfeit.* Manchester, NH: Sophia Institute Press, 2021.

Blai, Adam. *The Exorcism Files: True Stories of Demonic Possession.* Manchester, NH: Sophia Institute Press, 2022.

Blai, Adam. *The History of Exorcism.* Manchester, NH: Sophia Institute Press, 2023.

Brown, Raphael. *The Life of Mary as Seen by the Mystics.* Charlotte, NC: TAN Books, 2012.

Bukuras, Joe. "Exorcist Says Porn Addiction 'An Opening to the Demonic,' Despite German Priest's Controversial Denials." *Catholic News Agency.* December 1, 2022. https://www.catholic newsagency.com/news/252967/exorcist-says-porn-addiction -an-opening-to-the-demonic-despite-german-priest-s-contro versial-denials.

St. Catherine of Siena. *St. Catherine of Siena as Seen in Her Letters.* Translated by Vida D. Scudder. New York: E. P. Dutton and Co., 1905.

"Chaplet of Saint Michael." Knights of the Holy Eucharist. https:// www.knightsoftheholyeucharist.com/chaplet-of-saint-michael -prayer-download.

Clarke, A. M. *The Life of St. Francis Borgia.* London: Burns and Oates, Limited, 1894.

Council of Trent. "On the Invocation, Veneration, and Relics of Saints, and on Sacred Images." December 3–4, 1563. In *The Council of Trent,* edited and translated by J. Waterworth (London: Dolman, 1848). Available at www.papalencyclicals .net/councils/trent.htm.

D'Apolito, Alberto. *Padre Pio of Pietrelcina: Memories, Experiences, Testimonials.* Edizioni Padre Pio da Pietrelcina, 2013.

de Montfort, St. Louis. *True Devotion to Mary with Preparation for Total Consecration.* Charlotte, NC: TAN Books, 2010.

Dirvin, Joseph I., C.M. *Saint Catherine Labouré of the Miraculous Medal.* New York: Farrar, Straus and Cudahy Inc., 1958.

The Editors of Sophia Institute Press. *The Pope's Exorcist: 101 Questions about Fr. Gabriele Amorth.* Manchester, NH: Sophia Institute Press, 2022.

Eymard, St. Peter Julian. *The Real Presence: Eucharistic Meditations.* New York: Sentinel Press, 1938.

Ferrisi, Sabrina Arena. *Blessed Carlo Acutis: The Amazing Discovery of a Teenager in Heaven.* Cramerton, NC: Holy Heroes Books, 2022.

Forbing, Br. Raphael Forbing, O.P. "St. Dominic and the Ascension." *Dominicana Journal.* May 23, 2012. https://www.dominicanajournal.org/st-dominic-and-the-ascension.

Fraune, Charles D. *Slaying Dragons: What Exorcists See & What We Should Know.* Charlotte, NC: Slaying Dragons Press, 2019.

Fraune, Charles D. *The Occult Among Us: Exorcists and Former Occultists Expose the Nature of This Modern Evil.* Charlotte, NC: Slaying Dragons Press, 2024.

Ven. Fr. Germanus. *The Life of St. Gemma Galgani.* Translated by Fr. A. M. O'Sullivan, O.S.B. Charlotte, NC: TAN Books, 2012.

St. Gregory the Great. *The Life of St. Benedict: The Great Patriarch of the Western Monks.* Charlotte, NC: TAN Books, 2012.

Johnston, Francis W. *The Voices of the Saints: Counsels from the Saints to Bring Comfort and Guidance in Daily Living.* Charlotte, NC: TAN Books, 1986.

John Paul II. Encyclical letter *Redemptoris Mater.* March 25, 1987.

Kosloski, Philip. "5 Saints Who Were Exorcists." *Aleteia*. June 29, 2018. https://aleteia.org/2018/06/29/5-saints-who-were -exorcists.

Leo XIII. Encyclical letter *Quamquam Pluries*. August 15, 1889.

The Life of St. Alphonsus Liguori. Charlotte, NC: Slaying Dragons Press, 2024.

The Life of Saint Norbert, Founder of the Order of Prémontré. Translated by Rev. Theodore J. Antry, O.Praem. Tehachapi, CA: Bethlehem Priory of St. Joseph, 2021.

Liguori, St. Alphonsus. *A Christian's Rule of Life with Darts of Fire*. Charlotte, NC: Slaying Dragons Press, 2024.

Liguori, St. Alphonsus. *The Glories of Mary*. Charlotte, NC: TAN Books, 2012.

Liguori, St. Alphonsus. *The Great Means of Salvation and of Perfection*. Brooklyn, NY: Redemptorist Fathers, 1927.

Mansfield, Patti. "Blessed Elena Guerra: Apostle of the Holy Spirit." *Renewal Ministries*. May 24, 2022. https://www.renewal ministries.net/blessed-elena-guerra-apostle-of-the-holy -spirit/.

Menghi, Fr. Girolamo, OFM. *The Scourge of Demons*. Translated by Fr. Robert Nixon, O.S.B. Charlotte, NC: Slaying Dragons Press, 2025.

"Mother Teresa Acceptance Speech." The Nobel Prize. December 10, 1979. https://www.nobelprize.org/prizes/peace/1979 /teresa/acceptance-speech/.

"Mother Teresa Felt 'Tag of the Devil.'" *The Irish Times*. September 7, 2001. https://www.irishtimes.com/news/mother-teresa -felt-tag-of-the-devil-1.326164.

O'Brien, Fr. Bartholomew. *The Curé of Ars: Patron Saint of Parish Priests*. Charlotte, NC: TAN Books, 2012.

Olmstead, Bishop Thomas J. "Knees to Love Christ." *Catholic Culture.* https://www.catholicculture.org/culture/library/view .cfm?recnum=6378.

Pius XI. Decree *Apostolicorum in Missionibus.* December 14, 1927. Papal Encyclicals. https://www.papalencyclicals.net/pius11/ p11apost.htm. Translated from the Latin by Laura Bement.

Pius XI. Encyclical letter *Divini Illius Magistri.* December 31, 1929.

Pius XII. Encyclical letter *Mystici Corporis Christi.* June 29, 1943.

Poage, Fr. Godfrey, C.P. *St. Maria Goretti: In Garments All Red.* Charlotte, NC: TAN Books, 2012.

Pope St. Leo the Great. "Sermon 73," no. 4. In *Nicene and Post-Nicene Fathers, Second Series.* Translated by Charles Lett Feltoe. Edited by Philip Schaff and Henry Wace. Revised and edited for New Advent by Kevin Knight. http://www.newadvent .org/fathers/360373.htm.

Bl. Raymond of Capua. *The Life of St. Catherine of Sienna.* New York: P. J. Kenedy and Sons, 1862.

Reis, Sr. Bernadette Mary. "Padre Pio: 'If Only I Could Help You to Help Others, Jesus.'" *Vatican News.* March 18, 2018. https://www.vaticannews.va/en/pope/news/2018-03/pop e-francis-padre-piostigmata-confessor-healer.html.

Ripperger, Fr. Chad. "Exclusive Interview with Renowned Exorcist Fr. Chad Ripperger." Interview by Adrian Milag. April 18, 2024. Adrian Milag TV. YouTube. https://www.youtube .com/watch?v=jZYLWU4pvcs.

Ripperger, Fr. Chad. "Exorcisms: What Catholics Need to Know with Fr. Chad Ripperger." Interview by Chris Stefanick. April 10, 2022. Augustine Institute. YouTube.

Ripperger, Fr. Chad. "Fr. Ripperger's Wildest Range of Topics in One Show." September 18, 2024. Spiritual Strength with Gene Zannetti. YouTube. https://www.youtube.com /watch?v=gEKdA4xx6io&t=1942s.

Ripperger, Fr. Chad. "Levels of Spiritual Warfare & Our Lady." January 25, 2024. St. Patrick's Cathedral NYC. YouTube. https://www.youtube.com/watch?v=KQOSzZprIO4&t =2972s.

Ripperger, Fr. Chad. "Mary's Role in Spiritual Warfare." March 2, 2022. Full Sheen Ahead. YouTube. https://www.youtube.com /watch?v=ylHbccuHkTo.

Ripperger, Fr. Chad. "Our Lady of Sorrows and Healing," March 12, 2023. Sensus Fidelium. YouTube. https://www.youtube. com/watch?v=QqKV28eSaWo&t=2686s.

Rodrigues, Jose A. *The Book of Joseph: God's Chosen Father.* Toronto, ON: Ave Maria Centre of Peace, 2017.

The Roman Ritual, vol. 2, *Christian Burial, Exorcisms, Reserved Blessings, Etc.* Caritas Publishing, 2017.

"Rome's Exorcist Finding John Paul II Effective against Satan." *Catholic News Agency.* May 17, 2011. https://www.catholic newsagency.com/news/22558/romes-exorcist-finding-john -paul-ii-effective-against-satan.

Rossetti, Msgr. Stephen J. *Diary of an American Exorcist: Demons, Possession, and the Modern-Day Battle against Ancient Evil.* Manchester, NH: Sophia Institute Press, 2021.

Rossetti, Msgr. Stephen. "Exorcist Diary #176: Demons Hate Gemma." The St. Michael Center for Spiritual Renewal: Msgr. Rossetti's Blog. February 5, 2022. https://www.catholic exorcism.org/post/exorcist-diary-176-demons-hate-gemma.

Rossetti, Msgr. Stephen. "Exorcist Diary #302: Magdalene's Powerful Presence in an Exorcism." The St. Michael Center for Spiritual Renewal: Msgr. Rossetti's Blog. July 28, 2024.

https://www.catholicexorcism.org/post/exorcist-diary-302
-magdalene-s-powerful-presence-in-an-exorcism.

Rossetti, Msgr. Stephen. "Exorcist Diary #324: New Saint Helps Cast Out Demon." The St. Michael Center for Spiritual Renewal: Msgr. Rossetti's Blog. December 28, 2024. https://www.catholicexorcism.org/post/exorcist-diary-324-new-saint-helps-cast-out-demon.

"Saint Mary of Jesus Crucified." Carmelite Sisters of Ireland. https://www.carmelitesisters.ie/blessed-mary-of-jesus-crucified-miriam-baouardy/.

"Saint Quotes." Catholic Diocese of St. Petersburg. https://www.dosp.org/our-faith/saints/saint-quotes/.

St. John, Ambrose. *The Raccolta or Collection of Indulgenced Prayers & Good Works.* New York: Benziger Bros., 1910.

"St. Michael the Archangel." *Catholic Online.* https://www.catholic.org/saints/saint.php?saint_id=308.

"St. Norbert." *EWTN.* https://www.ewtn.com/catholicism/saints/norbert-712.

Sullivan, Msgr. John F. *The Externals of the Catholic Church: A Handbook of Catholic Usage.* New York: P. J. Kenedy and Sons, 1951.

Symonds, Kevin J. *Pope Leo XIII and the Prayer to St. Michael.* Boonville, NY: Preserving Christian Publications, 2018.

St. Teresa of Ávila. *The Life of St. Teresa of Jesus.* Translated by David Lewis. New York: Benziger Brothers, 1910.

St. Thérèse of Lisieux. *The Story of a Soul: The Autobiography of the Little Flower.* Charlotte, NC: TAN Books, 2010.

Rev. Thomas N. Taylor. *Saint Thérèse of Lisieux, The Little Flower of Jesus.* New York: P. J. Kenedy and Sons, 1930. Available at www.ewtn.com/catholicism/library/canonization-13797.

VanVickle, Dave. "Ep. 25: Rising Darkness: The Resurgence of Exorcism." Interview by B. T. Wallace. April 18, 2024. Truth & Shadow Podcast. YouTube. https://youtu.be/boSeVTuK Yqg?si=n4P99RPC8PoPXqQB.

Vatican Council II. Dogmatic Constitution on the Church *Lumen Gentium*. November 21, 1964.

Winowska, Maria. *Our Lady's Fool: Father Maximilian Kolbe*. Translated by Therese Plumereau. Westminster, MD: Newman Press, 1952.

Xavier, St. Francis. "The Prayer of a Child." In *The Letters and Instructions of Francis Xavier*. Translated by M. Joseph Costelloe, S.J. Brighton, MA: The Institute of Jesuit Sources, 1992. Quoted in *Magnificat* 26, no. 10 (December 2024): 55–56.

About the Authors

CHARLES D. FRAUNE holds a Master of Arts in Theology from the Christendom College Graduate School, as well as an Advanced Apostolic Catechetical Diploma. He has taught the Faith to nearly every age group over the past twenty years, from CCD to adult formation, spending ten of those years as a high school theology teacher. He also spent a few years in seminary formation before discerning that his calling was not to the priesthood. Charles is a husband and father, the founder of *Slaying Dragons Press*, and the author of six books, including *Slaying Dragons: What Exorcists See & What We Should Know*, *The Rise of the Occult: What Exorcists and Former Occultists Want You to Know*, and *The Occult Among Us: Exorcists and Former Occultists Expose the Nature of This Modern Evil*. His books carry the endorsements of prominent bishops and exorcists. You can visit his website at slayingdragonspress.com.

PATRICK O'HEARN is a husband and a father. He holds a master's degree in education from Franciscan University. He has authored or co-authored twelve books, including *Parents of the Saints*, *The Shepherd at the Crib and the Cross*, *Courtship of the Saints*, *The Grief of Dads* (co-author), *Go and Fear Nothing*, *Our Lady of Sorrows*, *Nursery of Heaven* (co-author), *The Truth about Hell* (co-author), *Saints*

Come in All Shapes and Sizes, Virtues of the Saints (co-author), and *Sacred Heart of Jesus.* He is also a contributor to Fr. Donald Calloway's book, *30 Day Eucharistic Revival.* You can visit his website at patrickrohearn.com.

Sophia Institute

Sophia Institute is a nonprofit institution that seeks to nurture the spiritual, moral, and cultural life of souls and to spread the gospel of Christ in conformity with the authentic teachings of the Roman Catholic Church.

Sophia Institute Press fulfills this mission by offering translations, reprints, and new publications that afford readers a rich source of the enduring wisdom of mankind.

Sophia Institute also operates the popular online resource CatholicExchange.com. *Catholic Exchange* provides world news from a Catholic perspective as well as daily devotionals and articles that will help readers to grow in holiness and live a life consistent with the teachings of the Church.

In 2013, Sophia Institute launched Sophia Teachers to renew and rebuild Catholic culture through service to Catholic education. With the goal of nurturing the spiritual, moral, and cultural life of souls, and an abiding respect for the role and work of teachers, we strive to provide materials and programs that are at once enlightening to the mind and ennobling to the heart; faithful and complete, as well as useful and practical.

Sophia Institute gratefully recognizes the Solidarity Association for preserving and encouraging the growth of our apostolate over the course of many years. Without their generous and timely support, this book would not be in your hands.

www.SophiaInstitute.com
www.CatholicExchange.com
www.SophiaTeachers.org

Sophia Institute Press® is a registered trademark of Sophia Institute. Sophia Institute is a tax-exempt institution as defined by the Internal Revenue Code, Section 501(c)(3). Tax ID 22-2548708.